Release Me!

Finding Joy Amid a Life Built from Rubble:
A Memoir

by
Leona P. Jackson, B.A.

To: Sherika
Thank you for your
Support!

H Jackson

Leona P. Jackson
01/16/20

Release Me!

Finding Joy Amid a Life Built from Rubble: A Memoir

© Copyright 2018 by Leona P. Jackson

ISBN-13: 978-1719400435
ISBN-10: 1719400431

Editing and cover design by Formidable Red Pen

Formatting by N.L. Gervasio

Published by RRR Books under the KDP imprint

Please direct all inquiries to the author: leonasbooks@gmail.com.

Printed in the USA

First Authorized Edition

Release Me!

Finding Joy Amid a Life Built from Rubble:
A Memoir

Contents

Foreword

I am honored to be asked to write the foreword for your first book, *Release Me!* Your dedicated effort to learning more about writing and then actually producing a finished book is a testament to your faith. I have an immeasurable amount of appreciation for the challenges you have faced and overcame.

Although your parents were not ideal parents I can't help but believe my grandmother, your mother, would be proud of your vast accomplishments. She would be especially proud of your writing skill. She too once had a desire for writing that was lost along her way. I could see your mother's admiration when you invited her to attend my fifth grade award ceremony, many years ago. It was my first and last opportunity to see her so filled with excitement and pride; as I walked to the stage to receive one certificate after another, half a dozen times or more, she rose to her feet and clapped *every time my name was called.* I remember thinking "Wow! She is proud of me." I believe her pride in me was an extension of her pride in you as a parent, as a daughter, as a decent human being. Thank you for your outstanding leadership as my mother, my friend, and my confidant.

Your book chronicles your life journey from a harsh, unsafe, un-nurturing childhood through the challenges of young adulthood, parenthood, and finally a stable life as a healthy, self-determining individual. You learned to heed those inner heavenly tugs as a means of making healthy life choices and recognizing your own soul's worth. Even while you were still battling the consequences of addiction, depression, and compulsion, your courageous determination to stop the damage and repair the harm changed our family's destiny. I learned so much watching you diligently manage your time and efforts as a mother, a community board member, and as a career woman working not just one but two full-time jobs.

You have proven through your perseverance that transformation is possible. It is my hope that sharing your story will lend hope to those who are similarly ensnared in activities and behaviors that deliver only ongoing misery.

Your many difficulties have brought you great wisdom, which you now willingly share with others as inspirational truths. You have done this even while you were dodging personal and professional storms. Your experience of being transformed from an *I can't* person to an *I can* person reminds me of the great words of the character Socrates from the book *Way of the Peaceful Warrior, a book that changes lives,* by Dan Millman. He said: "The secret of change is to focus all of your energy not on fighting the old but on building the new." You've demonstrated the effectiveness of that principle time and time again.

I once sat listening to you musing over the undeniable fact that having a role model to learn from would have been nice. You said you had decided to become your own role model. What a concept! Most people would never think of such a thing; you thought of it, and you've done it beautifully.

This book is but one of many new adventures I saw you tackle as you mastered one creative challenge after another.

First, you began your writing exercises by jotting down single words from fragmented thoughts. Later you moved on to crafting sentences, then to building paragraphs, entire pages, and—in time—chapters. From the aggregate of those many notes, scraps of paper, and messages to yourself accumulated a manuscript—a whole book! I have found much wisdom and hope in these pages. It is a privilege to lend my commentary to your work.

This book offers hope to those who, like you did, find themselves looking for a viable path to lead them away from endless hellish experiences. You had to do that, repeatedly, just to be reintroduced to more of the same day in and day out. I saw what a relief it was for you when the forces of misery finally introduced benevolent ways of learning. At last, my beloved mother learned to live her life in peace with God, others, and herself. Your story is the perfect road map for those individuals who desire to find healthier solutions for their everyday challenges. Those who enjoy a good read, or who enjoy learning via reading, as I do, will also find much to appreciate here.

One day in 1977, when I was only five years old, I heard you utter a very faint "maybe," an expression of hope that turned out to be the beginning of a journey to develop a healthy, well-rounded lifestyle. I watched as you trudged your way to a fulfilling and happy destiny over the next forty years. Your success in transcending your billowing burdens of heaviness and transforming them into heavenly pillows of joy and contentment tells me that you finally found remarkable ways of believing and living. Your life as you have lived it and as you are now living it is a testament to your innovative creativity and faith in action.

As have I listened to you reminisce over the years about your not-so-gentle childhood experiences, I have found it extraordinary that you were able to find forgiveness in your heart even before you could explain the process of forgiveness. You seem to me to have an innate ability to anesthetize painful thoughts of your past so you can move forward. I know you were set on breaking ancient cycles of self-pity, self-denial, and countless fear-based actions, behaviors, and limitations, and in my mind, you have accomplished this herculean task with dignity and grace.

Now you are sharing your story with the world. Falling back on your dogged persistence and resilience, you have gently painted your truth, and at the same time you have detailed a method for achieving win-win outcomes despite a lifetime of midnights of despair. I believe your story will propel readers into the spirit of "I, too, can do this." Those ensnared in endlessly deep pits of folly, dungeons of distractions, and comfort zones of masked misery will especially stand to benefit from learning of your successful escape from a bleak and destructive existence.

This book offers new ways to view old burdens, new ways to learn better problem-solving skills, and new ways to view and test untapped growth processes. This text is a virtual classroom for learning greater wisdom, enjoying light-hearted amusement, and finding truth and inspiration.

As a first-time author myself,[1] I know it is not an easy task to write a meaningful book; you have surely proven that it can be done if you act on your determination. You have produced an audience-friendly book which lays out the drama and trauma of your early life and then shifts into pages of contentment and gratitude.

Your book encourages your readers to courageously (even if fearfully) take their places at the table of self-development and find their own unique voices of confidence and divine purpose. You

---

[1] *Vietnam, PTSD, and Therapy: Survived All That!* (2012).

have shared how you chose to let go of what did not work and search for more effective skills. You put your *two fish and five loaves* message into action all during my childhood; now you are doing it again here, for the benefit of a much wider audience.

The many messages you have shared in these pages testify to the need for each of us to create our own role model, our own supportive self. Rock on with your program of self-discovery and deliverance!

To the Reader: My mom likes to keep herself motivated by posting inspiring quotes that express how she feels about the joy of finding the ability to move from an "I can't" belief system to an "I can do all things" position. One of her favorites is by Josiah G. Holland: "The mind grows by what it is fed."

This book is an invitation to those whose writing journeys may feel a bit overwhelming at first. I encourage you to use the lessons in this book to take your rightful place at the table of self-development and find your own voice and purpose. Some of us have gotten comfortable with the talk of going somewhere, but it's all just talk if we continue to let our fears tell us what to do, where to go, when to go, and what mask to wear during the trip. Leona has taken her *two fish and five loaves* message to a higher level of action and service by offering them to you as a tool to assist you in your own journey.

Leona's story demonstrates that through relentless perseverance and application of her grain of a mustard seed faith, she has truly tapped into a creative power that is much greater than she ever imagined.

As Leona reviewed her own parents' marriage, and their disinterest in education, she initially tried to take refuge from her challenges by following their lead. Eventually, though, she somehow saw how self-pity and closed-minded living could make a mockery of one's efforts to rise above difficulty and pursue a more fulfilling life journey. Each of the fifteen chapters here examines a different perspective of learning how to stop focusing on dilemmas, drama, tragedy, and insecurities, and instead learn how to find your own personal guide within yourself. Now it's your turn: *go for it!*

Wishing you success in your journey to find your best self,

~Secret Charles Ford, Ed.D.

Acknowledgements

I would like to thank the Almighty for restoring my life to one of influence, wonder, and purpose. I want to thank my two children, Richard and Secret, for their unfailing love and support, which carried me when nothing else would help. I am thankful for the many fragments of wisdom sprinkled here and there in my life, shared with me by kind souls I have encountered along my many paths of change. Ultimately, I am grateful for the divine gift of gratitude and grace, which has transformed my thinking and allowed me to meet my challenging circumstances head-on, and to conquer my fears and my weaknesses. I stand in awe and honor of my generations of champions. Learning from their struggles and my own has allowed me to embark upon building a meaningful life of limitless ingenuity, joyous inspiration, and extraordinary learning opportunities.

At the same time, my incremental steps, stages, and processes have allowed me to grow from my once great hindrances and learn the lessons I needed to learn in the time and place where I would be most receptive to them. These non-stop learning opportunities, clearly customized especially for me, allowed me (and still allow me) to benefit by learning from my daily experiences and then by benefitting from my new knowledge.

To the scores of remarkable individuals who took the time to share their counsel and warmth with me until my manuscript slowly materialized into a reality, I say "Thank you."

It is so gratifying to know that we are not alone on our individual journeys. Learning to be self-sufficient and to support myself emotionally and economically became essential to my survival quite early in my life. It took many years and more effort than I ever imagined possible, but my love for writing has at long last resurrected my long-buried sense of play, passion, and persistence. Writing this book has launched the next phase of my lifetime journey of change.

~Leona P. Jackson
December 2018

x

Dedication

This book is dedicated to my children
Richard and Secret,
to my grandchildren
– Jamal, Zechariah, Jerrehl, Marquis, Naamah and Imani –
and to my great-grandchildren
– Tre'Veonte, TaJine, A'lierja, and Gibril

Introduction

In order to finally live a life of genuine fulfillment, I've had to learn to let go of ineffective messages, modify useless behaviors, and create effective thinking skills. My early life was marked by severe deficiencies and failures by caregivers. These unfortunately led to my developing unhealthy behaviors that then led to my making poor life choices and creating difficult situations for myself. After much self-induced suffering, it became crystal clear to me one day that a complete examination of my flawed character was vitally important. Otherwise I would end up giving my life over to misery and repeated failure.

It took many years for me to understand that I had the capacity to change, but once I understood this, I also became willing to consider new systems of belief. Deep within, I craved a new way of living. It was difficult to shift my perspective from what was to what could be. I had to commit to making different choices if I was going to change into the kind of person I wanted to be.

I could hardly imagine making such changes. I had never been successful at being in charge of my own life, and I feared setting myself up for even more failure. I wrestled with this idea of commitment to change for many years.

Gradually, as I thought, and studied, and pondered, I realized that I had become more comfortable with the concept of personal growth: it became gradually more appealing and felt twice more rewarding than I had hoped.

I had once felt saturated with an overwhelming sense of dishonor, of personal shame. I had observed too much small-mindedness within my environment. I worried that I would forever be trapped trying to reconcile the conflict between the deeply negative and hurtful messages of my childhood and with the life-affirming positive messages I was seeking as an adult. I wanted to live a life filled with the promise of peace, contentment, maybe even happiness, and that thought became enormously energizing. I sought and began to practice behaviors I believed would gradually produce self-esteem, self-discipline, and self-confidence. I wanted some "happily-ever-after" life experiences.

I re-examined what I wanted for my life. What I learned was that a part of me faithfully worshipped my failed circumstances. I was accustomed to failure; it was normal. I knew how to fail. I was good at it. Another part of me was afraid of change, afraid to try something new. What if I tried to change and failed again? Wouldn't that prove that I was destined to be a failure? Why not just save time and *be* a failure now?

Still, I was determined not to make peace with my comfort zone of misery.

It was difficult, and I didn't always succeed, but I found – if I tried – I could fight off the mighty rush of self-defeating thoughts that had plagued me for so many years. It took a lot of practice, but now I am usually able to ignore or redirect such thoughts into productive action instead of allowing them to set up camp within my mind and heart.

Demanding thoughts from *The Madwomen in the Attic*[2] were in full swing and interfering constantly. They were directing and redirecting, instructing and reinstructing, and becoming more and more challenging by the day. There was something wrong with everything and everybody, including myself, long before I became an adult.

I believe these "women" were instrumental in driving me to succumb to my various addictions over the years. As I dug further to find explanations for my behavior, and ways to change it, I wondered how unconscious patterns of self-destructive thinking may have influenced me to make harmful choices. How could I have done this, over and over again, so willingly, without the slightest conscious intention?

Whenever I searched my mind and heart for an explanation or even just for additional understanding or self-awareness, a different question would attempt to squeeze in and demand my attention. That question: *Was it possible for someone as tormented as I felt to actually change, to really straighten out and lead a successful life, or was it merely a hopeless wish?*

---

[2] I am not speaking of the book by Gilbert and Gubar, from which I borrowed the title because it so aptly describes my situation, but rather I refer to the multiple and diverse "voices" or "personalities" in my head that for many years continually tried to influence my thoughts, choices, and behavior. Over time, these "women" had a profound impact on my life before I finally learned to understand and control their influence on me.

The answer to that question changed practically by the moment. Sometimes it was yes – change was possible; often it was no – don't waste your time. I eventually realized that the answer depended a lot on what kind of day I was having, or how I felt about myself when I asked the question. Rather than continue to ask the question, I decided to change the options. Instead of asking yes or no, I changed my thinking about what kind of person I desired to become. In the end, I was able to accept that my heavy, trauma-induced emotional and spiritual baggage was mine to either carry around, unchallenged and burdensome, or unpack and redistribute or discard. If I made the choice to unpack, I would also be free to select different coping tools to carry with me for use when I needed them.

Although I sensed the Almighty could work miracles in the lives of others, I was skeptical that His mighty powers were intended to work for me. I had a very difficult time believing in a power greater than myself, even though I actually thought very little of myself.

Thank God for many chances. For a long time, I focused on my outward appearance; that seemed very important, even though inwardly I felt completely inadequate and unworthy. I cultivated my outer appearance to hide my feelings of worthlessness and shame. I hid from everyone else my sense that no one else cared, not even – especially – my parents.

I was desperate to have a changed mind, but I did not know how to change it. Shedding sorrowful tears was as close as I had ever come to internal relief. Instead, I spent far too much effort camouflaging my discomfort, and hiding it from others.

I imagined having a complete spiritual makeover, not just adopting some scheming religious shroud that would indulge my natural inclination to hide behind it or beneath it in fear. I had always done everything I could to shield my awkwardness from myself, but no matter what I did, I was unsuccessful. I still felt inadequate, exposed. What I wanted was an injection of confidence that would last at least twenty-four hours. I yearned for my frozen emotions to awaken.

I finally understood that the spiritual makeover I craved had to come from me. I began to examine my actions, feelings, and thoughts. I didn't know how to let go of the only me I'd ever known. I didn't know which personal traits were worth retaining, and which ones to try to eliminate. I didn't trust myself to make these decisions, not without a coach. I didn't know any coaches.

I began my search there. I knew I needed a coach – someone who could at least give me some ideas about how to proceed in my quest. In 2010, I was introduced to a valuable coach. Finally, I had found someone who might be able to help me re-create myself.

So, we began working together. My deepest and greatest desire was to become more internally whole. I had to learn how to take effective steps, how to measure progress, how to be patient with the process. Through much trial and error, I discovered I had achieved some small growth.

Any growth at all was exciting. Visible growth, growth that others could see, was amazing to me.

Still, I could not envision the individual elements of self-empowerment as they applied to me. I certainly did not fully appreciate the commitment required to achieve my newly-identified objectives.

This memoir is the story of my journey of finally learning how to grasp innovative growth objectives as a way intentionally and purposefully of taking control of my personal, professional, and spiritual life, as a way of changing the things that could be changed.

Finally, after fighting through the process of identifying every trait about myself that I could think of, whether positive or negative, I understood that this inventory of *me* could become my road map. Since that time, and after a lot of soul searching, I have gained a better comprehension of these concepts:

> *To Understand Rather than to be Understood*
> *To Thine Own Self be True*
> *You Shall Know the Truth and the Truth Shall Set You Free*
> *Having the Wisdom to Know the Difference*

All of these ideas helped to steady and improve my mind and soul as I pursued my journey of self-discovery and growth. I learned I had to be willing to let go of whatever things were blocking my pathway to self-improvement.

As I worked and changed and learned, I wondered if I would ever be wise enough to know the difference between what I could change, and what I had to just accept. In 1977, a moment of clarity fused with an inkling of courage and transformed the course of my life.

What I found was that God had renewed my mind and straightened out my thinking. This occurred only after I had fumbled around at the foot of the cross too long and had lain by more pools of defeat than I deemed necessary. This experience is sometimes called hitting bottom. I would have preferred another way of learning humility. My ongoing tribulations often seemed unreal at best. I figured I had become emotionally and spiritually homeless, and I was in dire need of guidance beyond my understanding.

Disappointments soon became my platform of strength. I began to see, feel, and believe in a divine power. Soon, I became hungry and thirsty for honesty and self-respect. A solid degree of self-discipline made its way onto my overcrowded, self-centered, holier-than-thou agenda. I began to crave the ability to reach for self-honesty, self-determination, and self-appreciation without a tainted ego. Finally, boredom vanished, and lasting peace of mind was born.

Chapter 1 - The Blues of 1609 Brooklyn: 1953

Master of mercy, please help me to overcome my silent annoying misery.

I was born January 4, 1947. Growing up, the days when my parents were emotionally unavailable were the good days. By the time I reached adolescence, I had learned to act as if my toxic home environment did not bother me, even though it did bother me, tremendously.

As I became a young adult, I learned if I wanted to grow beyond the harsh reality of my childhood, I needed to learn how to live differently. Only then could I begin to truly live the life I wanted for myself.

Looking over the fundamentals I had missed in my early life, I was baffled. I had no idea where to start, and I could not easily make sense of what I had missed. I had trouble just identifying what was missing. I knew I had missed love, and acceptance, trust, and even the simple joy of feeling connected to other people. But did I need all of those things? Could I get by with just one or two of them? How could I know?

Learning how to live a meaningful life became my number one goal.

Many years later, I realized much of what I had missed as a child was the nurturing and encouragement I needed to become the best person I could be, to explore my talents and abilities, to try new things, and learn and grow from failure and success.

Even simple, basic respect for me as an individual was missing. *I didn't matter.* If I had disappeared, the only reason my parents might have noticed would have been because they enjoyed treating me so badly.

Although abusing me empowered my parents, it defeated me. I missed hearing, seeing, or feeling anything that might have made me feel valued, anything that might have helped me to understand that life was worth living.

When I was six years old, mere moments after I started attending public school, my parents started their own hauling business. Their primary customers were large retail establishments and hauling away their cast-offs required three or four outside employees and some of their children to perform the work. I worked for my parents in their hauling business from the time I was six until I was sixteen. I became a fulltime worker and a part time student. There was no warmth, no love, no nurturing, no affection, and no guidance. There was nothing that one might expect to be part of the growing up process of a young child. I didn't understand the world I lived in. I guess the idea of teaching your child basic coping skills missed our neighborhood. I worked all day and night. My siblings and I quickly learned firsthand what it meant to be a slave and to work in a forced labor environment. I had many questions about my situation, but "Why?" was the largest question in my mind. The best answer I could come up with was that as a child I was supposed to honor my parents. That's what the scripture said.

What I deeply missed in my childhood was the opportunity to be a child. As the years drifted by, I simply lost my natural ability to engage in childhood wonders. Reading, playing, running, yelling, and – most especially – the freedom of laughing, were all forbidden. Most of all, my natural curiosity was extinguished. What I finally realized was that the inquisitive child within us never fully loses its desire to play and be guided. As adults, though, we can have the best of both worlds: the ability to play and work, to think and interact. Balancing play and work requires emotional and intellectual maturity; it's not typically something a young child knows how to do; it's a skill that comes with practice.

After I reached adulthood, I would sometimes find myself whispering, "Thank you, invisible God" When I was feeling particularly grateful, or when events in my life produced an unexpected positive result, no matter how small.

I could not grasp the culturally coded salvation talk which I heard spoken around me daily. People would say things like

"Thank you God . . . for leading the way back" or "Thank you for your sacrifice on Calvary" or other similar expressions of gratitude. Those prayers did not have any meaning to me and brought little or no relief at the time. I felt as if I had been born into a family that functioned only in crisis mode, constantly on the verge of explosion, with no relief from the relentless abuse. For the first sixteen years of my life there was much talk of a God that was vengeful, jealous, and frightening. I was the seventh of thirteen children, a very large family. The strain of a new birth every year exerted uncompromising demands on the entire household.

By the time I was born, my mother was busy trying to juggle more than each day's demands for her time and dedication. Operating the home, supporting the hauling business, and attending to her husband surely became a bit much. I was on my own from the very earliest possible moment I can remember. I cautiously watched for clues of how to act within the established family hierarchy. For some reason beyond my understanding I began to think of my parents as gatekeepers quite early. My village comprised none other than my parents and my siblings.

My siblings seemed okay with waiting idly for their life scripts; I joined the idle wait, too. At the time, I didn't know whether it was safer to be blindly disobedient or blindly obedient. I can't say I feared my parents; I just felt it was not safe to not obey them. As I look back on it now, I realize that the key question in my mind was this: *Why is waiting to be delivered easier than taking steps to be delivered?*

No one ever hinted that I could become my own hero, or that I could at least try to help myself until someone else showed up to help me. On the other hand, I never had any reason to think someone else would show up to save me, either.

I attended elementary school in Kansas City, Missouri. The school was five blocks from where my family lived, on Sixteenth and Brooklyn, within walking distance of our home.

From the time I started elementary school in 1953, I was petrified, frightened beyond reason, why I didn't know. I remained fearful, filled with nervous tension, until I was thirty years old. My fears tormented and terrorized me morning, noon, and night. None of my siblings seemed to be bothered by the soul-killing environment we were being raised in. As time passed we were

3

without the sheer necessities of a healthy lifestyle. There were zero utilities and even less food.

It was as if I was trapped in a straitjacket of fear: I couldn't maneuver within it and I couldn't remove it. In spite of my terror, I discovered during my first three or four weeks of kindergarten, that I experienced a certain degree of contentment while I was at school. This was a very new feeling for me, one I had not encountered in my life at home.

I and my terror settled into my class routines as best as we could with my fears bullying me with every heartbeat. I'm not sure when I noticed my fears had taken over my mind. I remember being very cautious and quiet before I started to school. I was afraid of life and living. I seemed to live just to dodge my fears by any means necessary for the next twenty or thirty years.

My parents' hauling business bloomed. In the beginning, I worked for them after school. At age six I could out-work my parents. I only needed to observe on the process for a few minutes and then I would mimic what my mother was doing as the trash rolled up the conveyer belt of the famous department store.

The hauling routine of coming home from school in the kindergarten and being asked to get into the cab of the truck to begin the afternoon to late midnight hours became the norm. For the next eleven years we hauled trash from department stores, movie theaters, hotels, and drug stores. This routine didn't bother me too much the first two or three weeks. It was a relief to travel with my parents in the cool breeze of the September weather, riding for miles and miles from one place to another. My excitement was genuine; the business activities offered a sense of freedom from the extended long hours of sheer terror of being at school and not fitting in around the house.

During my earliest years, my mother always shopped for our back-to-school, Easter, and Christmas clothing. She would bring home the new outfits and spread them out for us to examine the day before the holiday. It was a glorious sight to see. The bedrooms were too small to display so many individual sets of clothing; therefore, the large living room looked just like a small clothing store on those three special days. Her neatly organized displays had given me hope in the beginning. New clothing and school supplies had symbolized we were actually loved in some otherwise unacknowledged way.

Having my new school supplies helped to distract me from my budding confusion and anxiety. The distraction was fleeting; I looked forward to my new school supplies for the first three years or so. The sixty-four-count box of colorful waxy art sticks charmed me.

The beautiful rainbow of blending colors made me somehow sense that life's many hideous challenges would soften and blend into some order someday, even though my present reality told quite a different story.

Sweet-aromas seeped from the school cafeteria each day, teasing my usually starving belly. The enticing smells reminded me of our home once upon a time, not too long ago. Exhilarated by the aromas coming from the cafeteria, I'd make my frantic wild dash home for a lunch that was no longer there. This continued throughout my elementary school days.

I learned early on to run errands in the community during my lunch breaks, to fight off the natural hunger pains from not eating before going to work or school. The errands never made me late returning back to school. I would assist the senior citizens. For some reason they didn't frighten me. Had my personal situation been more secure, I would probably have been afraid to be so bold around people I didn't know, but I somehow had figured out that I would have to fend for myself. My basic need for survival outweighed the kind of fear most young children have of strangers and unfamiliar surroundings.

Much later in life, I searched hard to find and reclaim small levels of childhood joy. I no longer could recall from my child-aged perspective the warmth and pleasures, not even one brief second of warm contentment. It had all vanished from my mind. The family environment had become too hostile far too soon.

It became harder and harder to even remember any moments of happiness or amusement. No matter how hard I tried, I could not recall any times when I had experienced actual cheery, childhood glee. I so badly wanted to believe I had enjoyed such moments, to feel deserving of laughter, fun, and happiness. If they had ever happened, and I do not believe they did, the child's merry-go-round of pleasures had disappeared from my life, music and all.

At the end of each school year, I was promoted to the next grade, without having gained any new knowledge. This advancement through school was the only consistent progression in my life.

The movement from one grade to another sent mixed messages to me. Being promoted told me I was moving forward in some way, even though I knew I wasn't learning anything in the classrooms. I assumed life would become more meaningful later. Even though I was just a child, I knew I shouldn't have been moved from grade to grade. I wasn't learning because I was absent so frequently; that much I knew. I also knew I was not in control. The adults were in control. I had no power. I had no say so in the matters of my life. I learned that the best thing I could do to protect myself was to stay silent and out of the way as best as I could. I could not undo the choices of the adults.

Even though I was uncomfortable living what I knew to be a lie, I had no idea of my other options. I was a captive in my own life, and this captivity relentlessly squeezed any joy or happiness out of my existence. I continually searched my own mind and my environment for answers and explanations about why my life was the way it was. I tried to take control of my inner compass when I was very young, but I lacked the knowledge, the skills, to be effective in coming up with answers that helped me understand or accept things as they were.

I had the ability to release my mind from its ongoing fears. I had a unique knack for behaving rationally even during difficult moments and years. This ability worked in my favor for a while, until I became too preoccupied with all the things around me that I could not control. Eventually, I could not pretend to be ok anymore; my behaviors became more and more irritating and I began to sense that some kind of mystical or spiritual adjustment might be needed. Finally, I released the notion that my life would or could become better.

I searched my soul for the splendor of hope that was promised by the scriptures. What I found instead was a feeling of emptiness that was hard to ignore. I was so traumatized by the religion-at-any-cost lifestyle my parents had forced on me that I felt sure I would live in distress forever. Over time, the emptiness grew into an ache, and that ache grew more intense and painful with every passing day.

In my young mind, I knew something was missing, but I didn't know what that might be. I would try to find or feel something within my heart, but all I could identify was a deep sense of self-loathing. I would try to forget each day, and yet when I wasn't working all I could do was replay the endless moments of unpleasant experiences over and over in my mind.

The longer my situation continued, the more confused and unhappy I became. I felt like I was constantly screaming, silently, from the relentless mental pain. I simply wasn't equipped with the ability to ignore or forget the neglect that was happening to me and all around me.

As I look back now, I can remember moments of laughter in my family, up through about age four. For the first few years, I believe my home life was relatively normal.

In the beginning, my mother spent her time taking great care of her family and home. On various living room tables, she had displayed figurines neatly placed within colorful five-inch starched and ruffled doilies. When the windows were open, the breeze seemed to encourage the long lace curtains to sway in a rhythmic dance routine. Modern furniture sat in the various rooms of the house. Bold gold picture frames held photographs of family members. In those photos everyone looked content. There were collectibles placed on three-tiered, antique, redwood corner shelves. Hints of care and effort were all over the place.

Our home at that time had running water, lights, and gas for cooking. I do not remember seeing any extra's like a coffee maker, a toaster, or any other small appliances that made life in the kitchen easier. We still had a Wringer washing machine and a scrub board for laundry and my mother still owned curtain stretchers that she would assemble in the backyard on Saturdays. My mother had been a wonderful cook and homemaker. Our kitchen was furnished with one large dinner table. We had breakfast and supper together around the table almost every day, but especially on Sundays. Dishes were hand-washed and towel dried. There was quality family time in some casual way. The girls' interactions with our mother involved mostly getting our hair shampooed on Saturday nights and pressed by our mother on Sunday morning before Sunday school. We attended church pretty much all day on Sundays. It seemed that when we as children began to use the upstairs for our sleeping quarters, those meals at the table downstairs ceased altogether. The family was growing, and life was changing at 1606 Park. This was our first home in the city, but as the family grew it had become too small. At the same time, the trash business had become larger than life itself and was far too demanding. This was the reason we had packed up and moved just across the alley to 1609 Brooklyn.

Mr. Trotter, our former next-door neighbor, loved to sit outside in the cool of the evenings, cleaning the catfish he'd caught earlier that day while listening to the sports station on the radio. Sometimes when the old man returned from his fishing trips he would give us one of the large live catfish he'd caught. It felt good to receive his gifts.

The old man kept his radio on the baseball station during the summer time. The soothing voices of the game announcer coming from the open upstairs window provided a sense of calm for me.

Many things changed without the slightest warnings during my childhood. Neighbors were there one minute and then gone the next, just gone. No one spoke of what happened to them. They were just not there anymore. I was not sure if they moved away or passed away.

One day the fisherman was there, and then he was gone. I remember missing the exuberant sports commentators' voices. I also missed the cheers, applause, and laughter from the crowds on the radio. We didn't have a television at that time. It seemed that our radio was always on either a baseball game or on The Paul Harvey Show.

It was very difficult to sort out what to say or not say. The desire for freedom to play was at the root of what I wanted to say most of the time. However, after only a very few seasons of being allowed to play childhood games, I had been forced into a life without social connection, laughter, or childlike chitchat. I could never comfortably figure out what to say. We had no opportunity to learn conversational skills; our days were filled with orders and commands from our parents. As all children do, we learned what was modeled for us. Although we always had a large family, there was very little interaction by way of conversation, competition, or friendship. I personally felt that we were all growing up as unknown enemies.

Before the shift in our family life from play to conscripted laborers, we had been allowed to have fun; we had played fun games in the backyard, amongst ourselves. Our play area in the back yard was off limits for neighborhood children. At the age of five, playing games, reciting nursery rhymes, and singing songs were my primary forms of entertainment. I remember loving those moments of spontaneous, childhood vitality. Freedom to play childhood games and sing songs was my soul's delight.

When I was seven or eight years old, I learned to run back and forth to the neighborhood corner store to purchase small treats. The race to complete my daily trips before the big truck pulled up to take me to work gave me goal. I collected empty pop bottles to trade in for cash, and then used that cash to buy myself whatever little things I could purchase with my earning: pop, popsicles, pickles, peppermint sticks, or a small brown bag of assorted penny candy. Keeping myself occupied this way made my life tolerable, but once I had made my purchases, my contentment vanished, I didn't know why. Why could contentment not remain for a longer time? Was it even possible? Since I couldn't hang onto my blissful moments of pleasure after purchasing my sweet treats, I learned to make more trips.

I do remember how much I loved the times when we attended a different pastor's church before we obtained our own. One church sponsored an annual picnic every year. The picnics were held at the famous Kansas City Swope Park. There were shelter houses and picnic grounds for what seemed like miles. The park was shaded by numerous extremely tall and ancient oak, pine, and walnut trees. The community squirrels hung around as if they too had been invited. They ran fearlessly to and fro, or stood observantly while holding whatever treasures they had most recently discovered. Mother Nature seemed much friendlier back then.

My mouth watered to see the large barbecue pits smoking. It was exhilarating to hear the fire crackling. The hot charcoal ashes turning red, white, and blue intrigued me. The sights, the energy, and the chatter somehow captivated me; it all seemed harmonious.

Shiny tin foil was loaded with many hamburger patties, hot dogs, and slabs of well-seasoned ribs. The fire had worked its magic; using various degrees of heat, it turned the silver tin foil black, cold, and old. That depressing sight was offset, though, by the vision of colorful shining cans of soda, all crammed into several giant galvanized tubs filled with crushed ice.

The shelter house at the park was swarming with church folks and the long picnic tables were overloaded with food. There were just too many people and too much friendly chatter. Usually I would avoid the large crowd by running or walking around the park. Intense, independent activity seemed to temporarily erase my nervous disposition. I'd have to keep trying to figure out what to do next to cope with the chaos as the grown folks meandered around ignoring us kids. I walked and ran a lot; it was hard to keep still.

Even the cake walks and sack races were more than I felt safe doing. I could never feel comfortable as a contestant, but I enjoyed being in the vicinity and watching. I liked cheering for the courageous winners and losers. Some sack jumpers fell on the first hop; others tumbled and stumbled, unable to coordinate their balance. As long as I could keep moving, I enjoyed all the activities that came with the picnics. But, when the event was over I was invariably overwhelmed by uneasiness. I cherished the memories of the fun I had on those one or two occasions. After I realized the picnics had ceased to be a part of our lives, I sensed an incalculable, deeply personal loss. The shift from having at least one blissful activity to anticipate, to a fulltime daily life of nothing but work, was a difficult trade-off.

My little mind would race uncontrollably to and fro, my thoughts changing from moment to moment. This particular brand of childhood enjoyment—a giant outdoor celebration with an abundance of food and entertainment—proved too difficult for me to wait for each year. The relatively few moments of contentment, of feeling like I belonged (even though I was profoundly uncomfortable interacting with others), of being acceptable despite my idiosyncrasies, became insufficient when I knew the fun itself could not last long and would soon vanish.

I have memories from when I was very young that tell me Christmas was a time of merriment, at least for a little while. The holidays brought happiness to our home. Sometime around age four or five, I remember seeing our Christmas tree all lit up in our home. My eyes were filled with wonder, but I did not feel the excitement. I don't know if I was too young to have any expectations, or if the decorations just held no meaning for me yet. Still, the voice of Mahalia Jackson, rising from the antique phonograph player, was heavenly. She would sing so angelically that I could hear her joy. I was content as long as Mahalia was singing. Between each song, my contentment left, but it returned as soon as the first sound of the next selection chimed in. Two of my favorite songs were "Let the Church Roll On" and "One of these Mornings." On one particular occasion, however, she was singing a Christmas carol.

My father was standing beside me, in the living room. First, we were just looking at the tree all lit-up. Someone turned the key of the wind-up toy tin man—I'm not sure who. The little toy man was walking with a suitcase in each hand, swinging his arms and legs left, right, left, right. My siblings were very interested in this toy, but for some reason, the excitement I needed to connect with the little tin toy or with my father's interaction with the toy and with us did not emerge. I stood there waiting for a clue of what to feel, but that clue never came. My mother was almost certainly busy in another part of the house; she would not have been too far away, but she wasn't in the room, so I couldn't turn to her for cues.

I couldn't be sure how to react, so I didn't react at all, and neither did my father. I am not sure why he didn't; perhaps my father was a social cripple who never grew up emotionally. As I remember him, my father was pretty much closed off to everyone, so I did not take it personally. As life passed by, he grew quieter, crueler, and angrier. It almost seemed as if we were in his way as kids; in the way of what I could not figure out.

The Christmas and Easter holidays both brought feelings of excitement and sadness. I am still not sure if what I felt then was happiness or innocent hysteria. The "after-the-holiday-blues," had become real for me by the time I was six years old. I began to detest the arrival of the holidays because it was just too difficult to go back to normal when they were over.

11

Sunday mornings were busy: Learning our Easter speeches while we worked was mandatory. Dressing up for the Easter program at church was bitter sweet. I hated standing in front of the church to say my speech, but I felt beautiful and confident when I was all dressed up in my new outfit. It gave me confidence, but I still didn't enjoy having all eyes focused on me. I remember feeling happy about wearing new and pretty clothes; if I could have just been left alone to enjoy the experience, life would have been great. Happiness was so simple for a brief season and the next thing I knew pleasures were difficult to come by and I felt that I was missing more than my share.

I still remember my cute, shiny, black patent leather, baby doll shoes. The shoes had one strap that wrapped around my leg just above my ankle. My little white socks had colorful lace ruffles stitched on the edge. My socks matched my dresses either in color or style or both. My white Easter gloves and bonnet gave me something to fidget with. I needed a distraction from something, but I was not sure what or why. I didn't know then that many little kids need distractions; I only knew I did. I felt abnormal, defective. I thought every other child was able to sit perfectly still and not fidget.

As each child in the family finished dressing and was ready for church services, it was our custom to sit on the couch and wait for everyone else to finish dressing. I am sure this was my mother's way of making sure we stayed clean and presentable until we got to church. Once we were all ready to go, we would ride off to church in our Model-T Ford and later our Cadillac. Owning a Cadillac seemed important to the grownups, even if we were all living under the umbrella of mistreatment. Three things my parents deemed as important: cars, trucks, and property.

Once we arrived at the church and I'd given my speech and returned to my seat on the bench with my family, I fell fast asleep. It seemed like I was under a spell to dismiss myself from reality as promptly as possible!

Midway through the service the entire row of us would be fast asleep. In later years, I could easily envision our family pew filled with the entire row of heads bobbing back and forth and slowly swaying right and left; what a sight! Sometimes my mother would shake the ones closest to her; it was her intent for us to wake up the others. I would wake up momentarily to see the entire row of my siblings asleep. Hard work and the lack of daily rest and care left me exhausted. Sometimes my head would fly backward while I was nodding, as if with just another inch my neck could have snapped. Our mother would be holding the newest addition to the family on her lap and nodding along sleepily with the rest of us.

Never mind the drowsiness in the meeting, or the anxiety from giving my speech, I still managed to feel some brief excitement on Easter Sunday, in my Easter outfits and all. I could not explain the revived feeling. It was a vague and very brief sense of joyfulness that came on those early Easter Sundays for me.

Although, the excitement was short lived, I knew it had been there just the same, that presence of childhood joy. Later, I didn't feel the same excitement. Everyone else seemed to be so happy, for extended periods of time, about the birth and resurrection of Jesus, but I did not have the same feelings. I felt empty. I eventually grew to understand that I simply did not have any feelings at all, about anything. It wasn't just that I did not have any great fervor about Jesus. The idea that "He Arose!" brought me no inspiration, and the Easter holidays came and went with no great investment on my part. Pretty soon, Easter was just another day for me, and so was Christmas.

Somehow, year after year, my disappointment at missing out on the joy and gladness that Easter and Christmas had once held for me became more than I wanted to bear. My emotions seemed paralyzed. I did not know the word "paralyzed" or what it meant. Much later in life, I learned that the abuse of working in the harsh weather and trash world, the deprivation, and the insensitive treatment from my parents, had left me numb to my core. This was possibly an innate response – my mind and body's way of coping with an impossible situation for my own protection. I felt nothing, but I knew I missed those feelings I once had, and I could not stop thinking about the excitement and cheer that had accompanied the arrival of holidays when I was younger. My memory of the details was gone, but I remembered the feelings and longed to recapture them. Endless debates ran through my mind about how to find that missing joy, and about trying to understand what was wrong with me that I could not feel or think about anything else except the feelings of happiness I had lost. Those internal debates were riddled with much confusion and muddled thinking.

Over time, it became increasingly more difficult for me to want to live for another three hundred and sixty-five days until the next holiday rolled around. How could I stop this new torment of gloom from lingering around in my mind day in and day out?

I can't say that I was suicidal at age six or seven. I did not know I had that option, and I can't say how I would have thought about it if I had known. What I did know was that I was numb. I did not want to live or die. I just wanted the uncomfortableness of the ugly trash lifestyle to go away. I toyed with the idea of running away millions of times, but always concluded that I might run into something still worse than the trash world existence I was living.

I learned to act as if it did not bother me. I know now that I was depressed, but all I knew then was that which had once been pleasurable was gone. I kept trying to sort the mess out in my head. It was getting more and more difficult to make sense out of the wait for the holidays to return again and again. The heavy strain of pretending to be excited and joyous was just too exhausting. I wanted to think about something else, but I could not. My thoughts would not rest regarding the emotional fading of Christmas and Easter.

I now believe it is a detriment to one's personal development if threads of enjoyment, gladness, and moderation are not woven into the fabric of a child's early experience. I was obsessed at the young age of six about the matter. By the time I was in the second grade, my holiday delight had long since vanished. I remember the moment when I realized that my inability to let it all go had turned into steeped misery. I remembered the tremendous mental struggle, and wishing, months later, that I could let go of my past holiday blues. I believe not being able to let go was my first real addiction. Searching through my mind to find some moment of glee was wearing me out.

Life had become dull, frightening, and downright cruel. For this reason, a great deal of what had previously been pleasant became tiring, yet I could not stop the search. It seemed that my only enjoyable moments were when my mind recalled the few happy events of past years. Happy moments in my early childhood soon came less and less until moments of enjoyment were no more. It became difficult to appreciate and experience happiness simultaneously. One day, it became impossible to hold on to what few happy and exhilarating moments did manage to sneak through into my bleak existence. Mostly, they were lost or went unobserved.

I cannot say now, because I do not know, but something happened to change my parents' financial and social standing. Everything that had once been "standard" seemed to vanish overnight.

My mother's every-two-week routine hair appointments had once made a big difference in her level of contentment with herself. She had always taken great care with her appearance. She had always seemed like a different person—a happier person— when she returned from her salon appointments. Her change had represented peace on earth and good will to me. I recognized when she no longer visited the salon every two weeks she had lost something. I missed her healthy, well defined hairstyles. Observable proof of her self-care had given me refreshing moments of comfort. To me, lack of self-care reflected a significant loss of the family's sense of well-being. When this loss became obvious to me (and I don't know how long it took for me to realize there had been a change), I was not sure I had the right to be happy anymore. Kindness, contentment, and affection were all missing and that made life unclear, confusing, and uncomfortable.

I was very much aware that the other families in the neighborhood lived differently than we did. I observed one family in particular. I deemed them normal. They seemed to have a system. The father was employed and seemed kind, communicative, and mild mannered. The mother was everything I wanted in a mother. She, too, was employed; she had a charming personality, and cared for her family. Their two girls were happy, loved, and seemed to be well-nurtured. The girls attended ballet, gymnastics and took piano lessons. They were in school every day. I remember the older girl being in my sixth grade class, she was also the school president. When this family moved away, my parents purchased their home.

As my family situation declined even further, it became common for our parents to buy us inexpensive shoes that were good for a one-time-only wear, if that. I could not understand the point. After the first use, the shoes simply disintegrated. Once the soles of the shoes begin to detach, they made a slap-slap-drag sound with each step. Soon the shoes totally unraveled, making it impossible to take normal steps. Each foot needed to be raised higher and higher to make the complete steps with the detached sole loosely hanging off its base. Sometimes the traffic lights changed while I was still in the middle of the crosswalk, but I knew I would trip and fall if I tried to walk faster.

Our family life began to follow the pattern of those shoes: it was already unraveling and falling apart, but then began sliding recklessly downhill, fast, when we moved across the alley to a larger house. The house may have been larger, but it was a "fixer-upper" (although the place never quite got fixed up).

Shortly after this move, in my own mind I began to call my parents my "gatekeepers." I can't say now why I came up with that name for them, as young as I was. Possibly I figured that gatekeepers controlled, and parents nurtured. Mine weren't nurturing, but they were definitely controlling. Everything had gone sour: life, living, the whole creation. Darkness prevailed in my little world even in broad daylight.

Verbal communication was non-existent within our home. The rules were never explained, yet somehow, they were understood. Body language and other nonverbal expressions were common. When our regular family outings ceased to happen, it became more and more difficult to remember any previous contentment. My parents' trash hauling business was not for the faint of heart, or for youngsters.

At nine years old I was simply horrified by life and living. The hauling business was dangerous and exhausting, even for grown-ups. It was taking its toll on me and I had many more years to go. Although no one ever said it out loud, I had noticed that all of the older siblings were either put out of the home by my dad or they married or ran away. Seeing all of this, I just figured sixteen was the cut off of the enslavement. I was right. At sixteen, I was no longer allowed to go to work with them. I was lost, and I had no idea how to function outside of the tightly controlled work world my parents had kept me in for so long.

Still, working in the hauling business kept me from thinking about my never-ending and everlasting companion, a companion that eventually became my enemy: fear.

As family fun activities decreased, beatings increased. It seemed that physical chastisement became the gatekeepers' new activity of pleasure. Maybe my parents thought beating us was a good distraction from the harsh daily toil and the unceasing disorder and abuse in our home. Even though I was just a kid, I could tell our dysfunctional home environment knew no limits.

A friend asked me recently if my parents were cruel, or violent, or just not inclined to talk to me. She wondered if I was able to meet their expectations, even though they didn't tell me what those expectations were. As I ponder the situation now, I believe I exceeded their expectations and they had no idea what to think of my power and will. I simply loved to work but I wanted to be rewarded in some way. Even at the young age of six or seven, I knew I wanted to hear "thank you" every now and then. I knew I wanted to be in my classroom seat or desk, learning what I needed to know to be a useful and functional human, even though being in school terrified me. I knew I wanted my utilities to be on so my body and my clothing could be washed and clean. I don't know if it was intentional, or if they even gave it that much thought; what I do know is my parents were cruel by default.

Chapter 2 - Insecurities Gone Wild: 1954

A desire for self-care was finally born

My small hands helped my parents purchase five neighborhood homes in the end. In the neighborhood where we lived, a lot of people were selling their homes and moving out. As soon as our neighbors made their decision to sell their homes, my parents purchased their property. Only three of the homes they purchased had back yards large enough for our huge trucks and the many piles of used and useless junk we reclaimed. My parents taught us to call it "recycled material" but I knew what the proper name was: *junk*.

After a while, climbing in and out of our many giant trucks became second nature to me, and became a way of life for my family When we weren't sleeping or eating, we were working.

Most of the time, all five back yards were filled with small mountains of various second-hand goods and recyclables. The enormous size of the assorted piles of junk sometimes took my breath away.

As surely as we built those mountains with our own hands, we also dismantled them, week after week, as the contents were sent off to their next destination. Thinking about the drudgery of picking apart the many piles of reclaimed items in the yards, I remember often secretly praying my "If there be a God" prayer, earnestly, under my breath. The daunting scenes in our backyards were beyond any reasonable person's comprehension. For a small youngster like me, they were formidable. It seemed as if my life had become a series of frightening and pointless grown- up activities.

During the early years of the business (the years when I was in kindergarten through third grades), we built extra-large piles and created even more piles of all types of salvage materials in our backyards. By the time I was in third grade we owned three or more houses, and it was a terrifying task to find a safe path through the back yards. The many piles, stacks, and barrels of recyclables far exceeded what was typical for a salvage yard. A large pile of cardboard that had been in one place in the morning may have disappeared by the afternoon, or new piles may have swollen to cover empty space where smaller pathways had been. By evening there would be more tall piles to avoid. I worried I could be lost forever as I walked around and between the piles of stuff on my way to climb up on another truck.

We only needed a few things to make our operation a real salvage yard: several large cranes, a weight scale, and a pay shack. Instead of using a crane, they would have us kids disassemble the large loads of stuff dumped into the main back yard straight from the big trucks. The stuff came from one or both of our two local larger-than-life thrift stores, and Neighbors would occasionally stroll over to see what was available. They'd buy a tea pot or some small insignificant items from the piles.

The main yard of 1609 Brooklyn was always filled with huge amounts of secondhand merchandise. Three or four cumbersome, extra-large trucks were parked in the alley when they were not in service. I still wanted to play but there was no space or time for play. I thought to myself time after time, "this way of living will be over someday." All I knew was *someday* was not coming fast enough. Each day seemed like time without an end.

Our daily morning routine was to get up early, about four-thirty. We would be awakened by my mother with an aggressive, shrieking, loud whisper, "Get up!"

A little later, in a more hellacious tone, she would yell, "Come on!" Proper time for sleep was not found anywhere near my childhood. Usually it seemed that we had just gone to bed not even two or three hours earlier, and we were on the road again. Many days it seemed that even getting proper rest was a sin among the saints in my family.

I trusted my parents. I was a natural when it came to being trusting. I trusted everyone except me. I know now that what my family was doing was not typical, and by current standards would have been considered unsafe, neglectful, and abusive ill reasoning. Every now and then I wondered if the former slaves knew something I didn't. Slaves had to endure their merciless positions; they had no other option, no safer choice. I felt like my life wasn't very different. I had no choice that I could see: I was a product of a hustling, hauling world. I felt I must obey my parents in order to stay safe from their vicious bouts of wrath.

My parents had crafted an economic method for supporting our family. It may not have been the best system for other families, but apparently it was the best they could do. I can only guess that, "If they knew better they would have done better, I once heard someone say.

It seemed that in those years, women were somehow expected to tolerate the demands of their husbands without complaint. Perhaps that's why my mother's conversation dwindled down to six words: "Get up," "Come on," "Let's go," and – in the end, "Hurry up."

As an innocent child, I had even fewer choices. Complaining would have earned me a beating at the very best, so I did as I was ordered. I watched my life take one pointless turn after another, going from relative contentment, security, and decency to upheaval, insecurity, and indecency. We went from prayer to no prayer, from attending church regularly to not going to church at all, from being sent to school regularly to not being allowed to attend school at all, from proper rest to no rest.

In time our specific names were no longer called. I think maybe my mother was just too tired, or overwhelmed, or lost. Or maybe she just expected everyone to respond without argument. To be safe, I always assumed I was included in her daily early-morning, mid-afternoon, and late night calls. Whenever I heard the words, "let's go," I instinctively knew I was included! Her general "Get up," calls were both demeaning and demoralizing. I had no choice but to do what she demanded, even when it seemed as though she cared less and less about making a better life for herself and her family.

At the time, I just asked myself "why" a lot. I never could come up with an answer that made any sense to me. Now I know that what I lived through was actually a paradigm shift. One moment I was a little kid, glad to be alive and working because I was terrified of school. The next moment, I was an enslaved and exploited kid who would rather be dead or in school. Both of these scenarios worked on my mind and my heart. While my home environment had its displeasures, the stress of it grew familiar. I knew what to expect, even if it was terrible. I knew how to avoid trouble, even if that meant more work and less sleep and rest for me. I had grown afraid of being out of my familiar territorial boundaries; even going to school had become a more terrifying experience. I wanted to learn, but I was afraid of being away from the harsh reality that was at home. In subconscious self-defense, I became an emotional robot. I had no feelings whatsoever. I was traumatized before I turned seven.

There was much pushing and shoving in the mornings. I scrambled to find a space for myself in one of the overcrowded makeshift rooms. I'd stand yawning and stretching for a moment, trying to awaken and process the early morning pandemonium. After a few minutes, I'd get my first wind and begin searching and grabbing for whatever food I could find to feed my undernourished body. I had no time for self-pity. We worked regardless of the weather. Sometimes it would be minus-zero in the winters, and well past hot, with scorching sun, in the summers. Nevertheless, we worked. It was what it was.

"Come on!" my mother would growl! Those words became her mantra.

As a matter of fact, "Come on!" was the extent of the one-sided dialogue we heard day in and day out. It was easier to humbly obey the demands of the gatekeepers; I reckoned that there were too many more years ahead of me to rebel, for I was only maybe six or seven. I surrendered.

Most of the time I was puzzled by my parents' decisions. I was too young to be able to talk about the difference between sane and insane, but even as a tiny child I could unconsciously sense the difference between the two. I knew precisely which category my family fell into. Did they honestly think this lifestyle was okay?

In those days, children were treated as property. Laws had to be passed to save the children.

[3] If there were laws to protect children at the time, they apparently did not cover our family. We did what we were told to do, when we were told to do it, or we suffered the consequences.

I became a speechless victim, a much-dominated little nobody. The harsh orders to "Come on" led to submissive, blind obedience to my masters. Our parents discussed grown folks' business only amongst themselves. As far as the details of our free labor assistance in their business, I never heard them speak of it at all. They never invited us to offer our opinion on the matter. Once upon a time, some adults gave looks that spoke louder than any words could have. It was a look that made one feel as if they had crossed an unseen, irreconcilable line. These days, some would call it "giving the evil eye."

As we rode to the mall on the first day of child slave labor in 1953, I had no idea this new process would repeat itself for the next eleven years. I had no way of knowing how hungry, tired, cold, hot, frightened, angry, and hurt I would be, or how uncaring, indifferent, and hateful my parents would become over that same period of time.

The first day of the hauling adventure, I was waiting for my parents to return to the cab of the truck. They had been gone so

---

[3] As Marvin Gaye would later sing:

I just want to ask a question
Who really cares?
To save a world in despair
There'll come a time, when the world won't be singin'
Flowers won't grow, bells won't be ringin'
Who really cares?
Who's willing to try to save a world
That's destined to die
When I look at the world it fills me with sorrow
Little children today are really gonna suffer tomorrow
Oh what a shame, such a bad way to live
All who is to blame, we can't stop livin'
Live, live for life
But let live everybody
Live life for the children
Oh, for the children
You see, let's save the children
Let's save all the children
Save the...

(From the album "What's Goin' On" (1971) by Marvin Gaye

long, and I had grown tired of waiting in the cab. After maybe an hour or so, I grew more restless. The truck was parked in the underground loading dock of a well-known five-and-dime store, Woolworths, at the mall. The cab of the truck was high from the ground for a little person. I carefully climbed down to reach the ground, where I sat for a while. I sat and played for a few long minutes. Restless again, I decided to walk toward the loading dock stairs. I climbed up several steps and saw my mother there. I thought she might come to me, but she didn't. I stood watching my mother for a while. Then it dawned on me: I was hungry. Neither of us said anything; we just exchanged visual cues. I paid attention to her, and slowly, reluctantly, joined in helping her remove boxes coming out from the giant rolling conveyor. I imitated what I saw my parents doing that day and kept doing it for the entirety of my childhood and my early youth.

We both were stuffing, pulling, pushing, stomping, kicking, shoving, tossing, turning, stooping, and twisting, without a word. We did whatever it took to get those boxes off the conveyor and onto the truck. The recycle storage room was located in the basement of the store. I believed we were surely ready to go home when my father walked up from the basement and turned the conveyor off. We loaded into the truck, and to my surprise he simply drove to the next place, and the next place after that. I learned that day after completing the labor at the five and dime store that there were at least thirty other places at the mall for which we were responsible. I was amazed that there were dozens of other establishments for us to service in the same enormous underground delivery and parking area.

We had started at one o'clock in the afternoon when I was retrieved from school; now it was close to midnight. My first day had exhausted me; no way could I have seen this being my reality for the next eleven years, but that's how it turned out.

From each loading dock, we gathered as much recyclable material as we could. We would save the various materials to be sold later. Our back yards became the holding space for everything we collected. Once all the pickup collection had been done, we would then begin our second shift, the unloading shift, no matter the time of day or night. We unloaded the trucks into piles of similar materials in our back yards.

As time passed by, all of our back yards were filled with everything imaginable and some things probably no one would dream of. From broken hot water tanks, to outdated safes, to tons of assorted junk: you name it, we had large quantities of it. While it may be true that one person's trash is another person's treasure, I saw all that junk in a totally different light, and I usually saw it at night!

The piles in the back yards grew and grew, and my parents seemed to lack the ability to know how much was enough. Even though the back yards were full and overflowing with junk and debris and broken versions of everything under the sun, we kept bring more. In the beginning, my parents would return home to pick up several of us after school let out for the day. I was a great worker from the very beginning, so I was always on the summons list. Later, as the years passed, I was allowed to attend school less and less, until by the time I was released from forced labor, I was attending very little. I was such a great asset in the business as a child manual labor worker that it worked against my getting a good basic education. I seemed to know what to do without being told, and I did it without a lot of fuss. I told myself, they could not do without my help, so I went to work full-time and school part-time. (quite infrequently, as it turned out)

The second company we began to service other than the mall was one of the world's largest distribution companies in the Midwest at the time. It was challenging in many ways. First, this was not a job for small kids. Second, the round-trip destinations would not allow us to return home in the morning to be on time for school. Third, we were already shorthanded; my mother and I were the only two real workers. There were two other siblings with us, but they were too small to be of any real help. They generally stood around, doing very little. They were mostly in the way. Fourth, my father decided not to help with the process at all other than to be the designated driver to and from the many large establishments we serviced. Of course, he was the adult. For the next ten years, he appointed himself as the designated driver. Four of us had to work harder and longer without his fifth set of hands. My parents employed over a half dozen outside workers to assist with the business. However, the business remained understaffed to the bitter end.

The distribution company was the largest single business of the forty plus businesses we serviced. We would service this one company before school and again late at night. The company operated with three shifts, five days a week.

I was in the third or fourth grade before I realized the plot was intentional to minimize our desire for wanting to attend school. All of the vast hardships seemed deliberate. Learning while at school was another matter altogether. I did not miss a lot of days in early elementary school, but I was tardy, tired, sleepy, and hungry every day. I had a difficult time trying to be pleasant and productive instead of angry and depressed. The relentlessly harsh lifestyle vexed me to no end.

By the sixth grade, I was absent three days a week and tardy the other two. When I was at school I was so sleepy and exhausted, all I could do was watch the hands on the clock high on the wall. The magic sound of the day was the loud bell that indicated it was time to go home. We would line up in sets of twos to march down the long hallway before bursting out of the exit doors into the schoolyard. Once outside, I enjoyed only a brief moment of freedom. As fast as I embraced a gasp of fresh, free air, thoughts of my pre-arranged reality snatched my freedom away. All that awaited me at home was dangerous and toxic enslavement.

Although, I had opened my little books and tried to read aloud when called upon in the first grade, I could not retain any of the contexts or understand the content of what I was "reading," let alone build toward the next reading level. In all the years that passed from the time I entered Kindergarten until I was released from involuntary servitude, I had not comprehended a single piece of information from sitting in school classrooms.

At the elementary school, there was a jungle gym on the school grounds. This was my favorite place to wander; I could play alone and not feel bad. I did not know how to mix with other children, or maybe I didn't want to mix with the other children, or perhaps they did not want to play with me. I did not know which the real case was, and I was too fatigued to care. My mind was tied up with the never-ending demands of the hauling business at home. I didn't have the energy to think about how to navigate schoolyard relationships with my peers.

During the school break each summer my fears seemed to vanish, but as soon as the school term began my fears would return again. I was never sure how fear found me, but it refused to leave me alone. It seemed to go to sleep with me and wake up with me. Feeling like a misfit sometimes took the place of fear. I could not tell which was worse, the internal or external conflicts.

In the beginning, my parents would return home from their daytime toils to pick up several of us youngsters after we had come home from school.

My mother would hobble into the house and shout, "We are ready to go." Several of us would scurry out of the house. During the winter months, this meant we were leaving the house as night was falling. During the early morning we couldn't see my parents, or the trucks, because there were no lights in the back of the house where the trucks were parked. Instead, we would follow the noisy hum of the truck's motor until we found the vehicle where the adults were waiting inside of the chosen truck within the darkness.

Once we found the truck, we'd pile into the cab and position ourselves for the long ride. Sometimes we would sing as we traveled between our many stops, one song after another. Maybe that's where I learned to take comfort in music.

Somewhere along the way I stumbled upon the words "My dreams need to be greater than my circumstances." I could not imagine how any dream could be greater than this perpetual madness, but the words never left me. Later I came to understand that "greater than" meant "capable of inspiring me to rise above" my circumstances. When I finally understood that concept, I was able to start dreaming of a different kind of life for myself.

At some point during the hauling years, I also stumbled across a line from Shakespeare's "Hamlet" that gnawed at me: "There is rest in silence." This idea was even more perplexing than the idea of anything being "greater" than my circumstances. There was not any rest in silence for me. As a matter of fact, I could not shut my mind off. There were too many arguments, questions, and a persistent, fanatical need hanging around in my head to condemn others and myself.

There was no time for proper rest or sleep. No time for nourishing food. No time for developing healthy social skills or learning coping methods or useful behaviors. No time for developing healthy psychosocial skills. No time for academic education. No time for play and certainly no time for encouragement. My basic blueprint of life seemed fatally flawed.

In the early days when we were not allowed to attend school, my parents would stop by a grocery store whenever they could not persuade us to wait any longer to eat again. They would return shortly with a small grocery bag of foodstuff. In the brown paper bag there would be enough food for one or two of us. Four or five of us stood in a circle, eagerly awaiting our simplistic feast. With a child's innocent outstretched hand, I would claim the limited items pushed my way. The food offers were particularly challenging, and emotionally devastating. We were rarely fed an actual meal, and almost never given an amount sufficient to fight off hunger.

I learned to live with the many complications that defined my existence. For instance, if neglect was my reality, I managed to find ways to not let the truth of neglect own me. If being ignored was my fate, I learned to not let being overlooked mirror my collective truths.

There seemed to be some kind of system to the manmade madness, but I could not figure out what was causing the madness in the first place. I could not sort out the labor madness from the living madness or the school madness. About age eleven, my emotional development generated yet another complex struggle within: I became preoccupied with thinking about whether I should jump off the truck and run away. The idea was deeply appealing. I was physically and emotionally miserable. But I was also aware that running away could cause more problems than it would solve. Knowing that running away could cause problems also meant I was always more concerned about what conditions I'd be running to, rather than what conditions I would be running from, so I stayed. I stayed in the known misery rather than chance the unknown.

Warm tears kept me from going totally insane; I cried a lot. I cried and prayed while I worked, and when I was finally allowed to rest between one place and the next place to be serviced. I cried because of the *Father forgive them because they knew not what they do* sensation I felt. And maybe they did know. I didn't know what was true. I cried because the agony and pressure were ultimately unbearable; I cried because they were my parents, my role models, and my gatekeepers.

It was an awful, dark life, entering dark sheds, working through the dark nights, rising in the dark mornings, laboring through dark and freezing cold winters, and sweating through unbearably hot and sweltering summer days and dark nights. When we arrived back at our dwelling after a work shift in the winter time, we would stand by the old coal stove to thaw our frozen fingers and toes. The first five or ten minutes of the thawing process were the godawful worst. Although we had dressed prepared for the harsh winters with hoods, stocking caps, gloves, two or three pairs of pants and shirts, and even men's brogan boots with maybe two pairs of thick socks, the long working hours in the wet, falling snow meant no amount of clothing was sufficient. In the end, we were cold and frozen from being in the harsh elements for long, seemingly endless, hours of backbreaking work.

I prayed and sang a lot. I needed and wanted God's help. I thought if I could just claim some of God's amazing grace, I would be all right. I held onto that thought tenaciously, relentlessly, and ceaselessly. I repeated it in my head: "I need some of that amazing grace." I had not a clue of what amazing grace was but because I knew I needed something, I did not know what else to want at that time.

Sometime later, I began to understand that I was so desperate for divine intervention that I had taken my desperation to be faith. I believed if I thought about it long enough and intently enough, it would happen. I also mistook my own stubborn will for spiritual power, with the same pattern and goal in mind: if I willed it long enough and hard enough, it would happen. My inability to genuinely connect with that source of omnipotent presence and power was so vexing.

It was past agonizing to work so hard from early in the morning until late into the night. Each day, I awoke with the hope that we would finish in time for me to go to school. After a while, I learned that dangling the hope of going to school in front of me, like a carrot being hung in front of a horse, was a hoax to keep me working harder and willingly. That hope made me more dedicated and got me to work harder and more rapidly. The voracious nature of the hauling beast ruled day and night. Crying, praying, and singing were the only tools I had to relieve the suffocating heaviness I felt. At first, I played various mental games to help myself withstand the brutal physical work. My imagination played a vital part in surviving the hardship long-term. By the end, I'd invented a scenario where I'd get some large settlement at sixteen, when this trial was over, much like some people envision winning the lottery.

In the beginning, as a little child, I was somewhat fascinated with some of the activities of the hauling business. The kicking, stomping, and ripping of each box created a captivating rhythm. When we all worked together at the same task, there were five sets of fists and hands beating and punching in time with a cadence dictated by the conveyor belts.

It's difficult to describe all the different variations of the many sounds from tearing the four sides of cardboard boxes by kicking, splitting, popping, and banging with our hands and feet. When we punched and pulled with our little fists or kicked with our little feet, there seemed to me to be a beat. There was a unified rhyme, rhythm, and wordless beat, just eight hands and eight feet physically flattening and stacking mini piles of boxes to be snatched up and tossed into the truck bed sporadically. The super-fast production process created a harmonious tempo of an on beat one minute and off beat the next, the sound intrigued me, as a child. I finally noticed that my vigorous actions moved the mundane, daunting, laboring truth farther and farther back within my mind, day by day. It was like a boxy harmony. All of the commotion kept my fears and tears at bay, at least sometimes.

Despite the musical, artistic rhythm of the work, manually tearing the four corners of each box with our bare hands was a cold skill. We would rip the corners with our bare hands while simultaneously kicking the corners out of another box with our feet, bam, bam, bam, bam. Eight corners surrendering their standing positions at once. There were twenty or thirty flattened boxes per pile. Another child would do nothing but toss stacks onto the truck after a while. Tearing boxes, throwing stacks into the bed of the truck, dashing into the truck, and arranging the wanted recycling from the unwanted recycling was a skill. I was the mover and shaker most of the time. In the early days it was an interesting scene for a kid. The more boxes we ripped up, the more fell from the high conveyor at the distribution company.

The musical, rhythmic beat helped me to focus. As we worked we picked up the pace as if we were having a contest for who could work the fastest. This process kept my mind energized and occupied as I worked and helped to keep my thoughts off of the pain and fear that accompanied the work. The child in me was proud to be the best worker, despite the fear and fatigue. The contrast between difficulty and success may have inspired me, but it also confused my young mind.

I do not remember when I learned to pray, but I remember praying continuously from a very young age. Apparently, my need for comfort and hope translated into reliance on prayer, a frame of mind which came to me easily somehow. Praying, whether reciting memorized prayers or uttering random pleas for protection and assistance seemed to help buffer me from the harsh emotional and physical reality in which I was living. Praying, singing, and crying seemed to give me the strength for enduring my battles against the unbeatable foe.

The first winter was probably the worst of the eleven year stretch. I hoped the vicious weather conditions would persuade my parents to think otherwise about their commitment. I thought the malicious freezing sleet and snow storms, pounding hailstorms, sweeping rain, and howling wind storms presented a convincing case against working outdoors, and in cold sheds, loading docks and unheated warehouses. I was wrong. Since we were a nonverbal family, they could not hear my silent, humble pleas. I did not say anything or tell anyone about my idea that the weather should be considered before we were demanded to work for long periods of time outside. I'm sure I kept my mouth shut to avoid any punishment that might result from my complaints. Anyone who dared to comment was immediately labelled by the old folks as a "know it all." If the harsh weather alone could not persuade my parents to change their unrealistic outlook, nothing I might have said would have made any difference.

Looking back, I recall working through various winter snowstorms, spring thunderstorms, autumn dust storms, and the heat of cruel hot summers, I realize that I was in the hands of mercy the entire time. I was protected, although as a child I had no way of understanding the part mercy played in my survival. Just as I mentioned about grace I also knew absolutely nothing about grace, I knew even less about mercy. The only thing I knew at some point in my life was that if I survived that manner of mental illness then it would be a miracle. Most of my understanding of grace and mercy came from surviving the times and facing similar situations as an adult later on in my life.

Some of the cardboard boxes I opened were stuffed with layers of plastic bubble wrap. The plastic air-tight bubbles got my attention every time. I would stop working for a little trivial entertainment; my little fingers had a bubble wrap stress relief workout. I would pop the little bubbles with my fingertips and delight in the popping sounds. I thought they were sensational. Although my bubble wrap recesses only lasted but for a few seconds, they created some homemade fun. Between the uncompromising weather and the horrible, life-sucking, recycling processes, I had to take my amusement wherever I could get it. It may seem unimportant to get excited about popping a bit of bubble wrap, but I believe I was trying to keep from going insane. It was another form of accepting the things I could not change.

In the 1950s, the shopping mall in Kansas City was one of the largest and most enchanting malls in the world. In 1953, this mall, or the underbelly of the mall, became the location of my parents' new career in trash hauling. It became my new prison. The mall had one day thrilled me and the very next day it vexed me. The mall's vastness and variety of stores became daunting to me on the second day of "service." Never mind the Christmas lights, the music, and the decorations: the wonderful shopping mall in one day's time became came one of my worst nightmares.

The first winter of working to clear the mall of its unwanted leftovers was a wakeup call: I had thought that working all hours might give me some respite from my school fears. In fact, the work was so demanding that I did not have time to worry about my school fears. I was hungry, angry, lonely, and tired every moment I was working. My school fears became secondary. I worried that I would not survive the exploitation from my parents. I had no relief from the constant anxiety, fear, and server neglect.

That first winter added new dimensions to my previous apprehension. I had believed working through that first brutal midwest winter would convince my parents to release me from my hauling duties, at least when the weather was extreme. I was sure being outside for long hours in the drizzling cold or scorching hot sun would certainly convince them that this was not a child-friendly work environment. I was wrong. If there were forecast warnings, my parents ignored them. Clearly the comfort and safety of their children was only a minor concern, or perhaps no concern at all.

The business gradually took over every aspect of our lives. They kept adding more locations for us to service, beyond the mall, so it was physically impossible to take care of them all in one twenty-four hour period.

During that first Christmas holiday season, the music blared from the outside PA system at each of the eight drug stores we serviced around town. The stores were located miles apart in various areas of the city. We were damn near frozen by the time we made our way from one store to the next. I would try to distract myself from the miserable cold and the terrible work by attempting to focus my mind on the holiday music. There was not any merriment in the work regardless of the season; I'd spend my time trying to distract my mind from the labor and the weather, and the hunger, and only God knew what else.

I sometimes wondered what life was like for the many excited shoppers. Every now and then while toiling I would glance around to take in the details of my surroundings. Heavy layers of glistening snow captured my attention. The sight of it added to my already debilitating misery. Sometimes the cold, gusting wind would take my breath away as it swirled first one way and then another around my frozen cold face. When every inch of the landscape was covered with snow, the scene reminded me of images of the ice-cold North Pole I had seen on television. As beautiful as the scenery was, these harsh, cold scenes looked more and more treacherous, unsympathetic, and uncompromising the longer we labored. As the night darkness crept closer toward the early morning hours, sometimes I felt that the snowflakes and the coldness were saying to me "just deal with it, child!" I was a young girl. I had no way of knowing how to deal with this harsh reality other than to just keep humming and working as fast as I could before my fingers and toes froze stiff, especially during the later winter night work hours.

The first twenty or thirty minutes of the work shift were slightly more tolerable than the rest. After we had been working for a short while, between the painfully piercing cold days and nights and the tortuous recycling work, I had to quit thinking about any physical impact at all, just so I could keep going. As we worked later into the night, we would still be stomping and smashing away after the store had closed. The outside parking lot flood lights were turned off and all the other workers gone home. Left alone in the dark and cold with my completely indifferent gatekeeper, I intuitively knew we lived outside the boundaries of healthful living. I longed to be grown up and demonstrate to my parents how to care for children the proper way.

As shoppers walked quickly to and from their cars to avoid being frostbitten, I would make quick mental notes of our work progress from the time they dashed into the store until the moment they returned to their cars. Many such leaving-and-returning scenes allowed me to distract myself from my own agony. Our horrific, relentless, grueling recycling escapades made me shiver with despair. I would face each new challenge of recycling agony minute by minute, hour by hour, day by day, year by year, and place by place. It was all I could do to keep from going totally insane.

My parents seemed to believe that anything fun was a sin, although they never said these exact words. The way I viewed the situation, our parents made our lives one living hell on earth single-mindedly and singlehandedly. The severity, the harsh work certainly could never have been described as fun, and – if hell is anything like it has been described by some religious people – a decade of a trash hauling lifestyle certainly would redeem me from a multitude of sins.

After my parents entered the hauling business, there was no looking back. We no longer fit into the social place we had tried to occupy previously. I concluded that values, morals, healthy standards, and safety were for others, not us. It was difficult to make peace with that belief, so I kept thinking there had to be a better way of living for me!

My parents made sure I was always included in their daily recruitment of workers. I was with them each day before school, after school, and finally during school hours. I believe, in the beginning at least, the reason they took me and my next younger sister with them every day was simply for lack of a babysitter. My sister and I were in the same morning kindergarten class, and there were no other siblings to stay at home with us after we walked home from school.

How they came to believe that I, their fourth daughter and seventh child, was essential to their success for the next ten years I will never know. I had a great zeal for being occupied, even at age six, but I could certainly have been just as well occupied with education and learning. Instead, I was climbing in and out of giant vehicles and hanging around dangerous machinery, and breaking down hundreds and hundreds of cardboard boxes, day in and day out.

I was not allowed to begin school until the autumn of 1953, even though I had turned five on January 4, 1952. My education was clearly a lower priority as far as my parents were concerned. They were more interested in the different ways they could put me to work. My obsessive performance came in handy when I was asked to assist with shoveling hot burned coal at the foundry and unloading multiple boxcars of coke and pig iron. If they could get me to do it, that meant they didn't have to do it all by themselves or pay some other adult to do it for them.

It was difficult to tell if they had a hidden motive and conveniently made going to school too complicated for me to continue to desire going. It became more of a hassle to want to go to school and be denied than to continue wishing and hoping and be disappointed daily. We hadn't been in the hauling business for more than a couple of years before our school attendance became only a minor issue. Before much more time passed, it became totally unnecessary as far as my parents were concerned.

I remember the day when finally, one of my parents announced, "No one is going to school today." Our home had caught fire and there had been more smoke damage than structural damage. We still lived in the damaged house, but my father was sleeping at the church across the alley. Why he was doing this, I never knew. While we were all there for some reason, my father had sat up on a pew in the back of the church and made his announcement. He sat up, said what he said, and then I am not sure if he stayed or left.

The Red Cross had supplied clothing for us. I was excited, for it had been a long time since I had received something new, not even school supplies. There was no excuse to keep me from going to school otherwise; the excuse was that we all had to go to work. I was sentenced to a life of hell at that moment. I changed back to my old raggedy clothes and returned to the truck for our departure. I was stunned when I heard the words, "No one is going to school today."

Prior to hearing those words, I had resolved to work as fast as I could to complete the early-morning job at the distribution company, hoping I could run to school when we were finished. I knew full well I was going to be tardy. It seemed that no matter how hard and fast I worked, I still did not make it to school most of the time; we didn't even get there in time to be tardy. The extra-large amount of physical work demanded of my mother and me was too much. Once the early morning distribution task was completed, we'd roll down the giant, overhead, loading dock door. We would then tie a large tarp over the open top trucks, killing more precious time. When the truck was ready, my father would wake up from napping in the cab of the truck and drive us to the next destination, just like that. Sometimes, if I was lucky, we might get done early and I would be allowed to go to school, but I was always late. I learned to tolerate being tardy as opposed to being absent.

I was sure my father would drive as relaxed as he could, intentionally getting stuck at traffic lights, just to make sure it would be too late for me to try to attend school. Eventually, I just accepted that I would not be going to school as I so wanted too. I was in the six or seventh grade now. When we arrived at one of the eight drug stores to be serviced, instead of going home or dropping me off at home after leaving the distributing company, I would be past mortified. I wanted to go to school now. It seemed unreal to not be in some teacher's classroom, feeling scared and out of place.

At the time, I did not give a lot of thought to why my older siblings were not chosen to work in the hauling business. Later, however, I tried to figure out why I felt so dedicated to the cause. My inquisitiveness became a dangerous distraction for my safety around the large trucks, equipment, and junk.

I remember my oldest brother working with us for a very short time. Soon, the older two brothers had their own individual large trucks and routes, and they were salaried employees within the King's Hauling Business. I only remember the third brother helping to unload the boxcars at the foundry; he did that exactly once.

My oldest sister had taken over my mother's small ironing business. I never was clear why the next sister was not chosen to help out within the ironing or hauling business, but I did notice when she would go with us, she was not inclined to participate in the labor-intensive work activities at all. The next sister in chronological order took over my mothers' household duties: washing, cleaning, cooking, and caring for any new additions to the family.

I noticed each year I had more and more fears at school and at home. The working activities helped my fears to not get the best of my mind or get in my way of being highly productive. I can't say why I was required to work so relentlessly in the family's hauling business. Even the initial need for a babysitter was no longer an excuse after a couple of years. I had a difficult time accepting the fact that attending school regularly was not an option for me. I am not sure why the three older girls were not asked, as I was, to be an on-going part of the hauling business. It seemed to me that they could work just as well as I could, if not all the time at least every now and then. From six to sixteen, I just lost interest in trying to make sense of the way family decisions were made.

When I was busy I did not think about how frightened and out of place I felt. I internalized my discomforts and fears far too deeply. I truly felt there was only one way out; I simply had to wait until I turned sixteen, and I had to find a way to be okay with that knowledge. Sure enough, at age sixteen I was sent off to beauty school, which was their way of dismissing me from the business. I then noticed my fears seemed linked to every breath I took. My mind continued to search for any possible avenues to divorce, escape, or separate myself from my past inhumane situation. I was trapped in a silent world of disbelief. It was a state of mind without any comprehension, without the ability to let go of what my life used to be like. I lacked the ability to free myself from the mighty grip of paranoia and panic.

While I was neither the oldest female child nor the youngest, I possessed unusual laboring stamina. I grew to be an *all work and no play adolescent*. I had missed *playing* from age six to maybe eight and finally I noticed as long as I was busy, I could not tell the difference; working had become an activity that satisfied something within me.

At twenty one, I finally realized *fear was my supernatural master*. I often wondered how I'd been caught in the snares of my disquieting, fear-based life. I would look at my siblings and my parents, hoping to see or hear clues about how to match their apparent feelings of liberty, independence, and esteem. Somehow, they seemed at peace living within our chaotic, fear-based family culture. I saw nothing. I could not see how they could stay so calm while I was constantly distraught. I began to believe there was something wrong with me. I could not accept the way things were and I could not overcome my feelings of helplessness.

Several of my siblings found laughter some way, somehow, all during the day when I was in their company. A lot of the time, my different behavior was the target of unpleasant giggles from them. My experience is a real testament to the principle that "negative attention was *not* better than any attention at all." I always wondered how the mistreatment they inflicted on me could have been justified or tolerated by our parents. Weren't they supposed to protect me from the aggressions of larger, stronger people (even larger, stronger siblings)?

Their constant failure to ensure my safety was all the proof I needed that no one was going to protect me. It was proof that our way of life would go unchallenged by anyone – family, friends, schools, religious leaders, or municipal authorities. The dysfunction would be tolerated without the examination, investigation, or modification by the professional authorities. I was trapped, doomed to an existence that I could not control, condemned to a life that placed me in peril from one moment to the next.

This realization also taught me something else that I didn't understand until much later in life: our obsessions can be either healthy or unhealthy, and it is up to each person to determine how to break obsessive struggles.

I sometimes now think that it may have been my destiny to learn how to adapt so early in my life; my childhood strength and energy somehow has blessed me. I learned to enjoy working immensely. I am not so sure where I get the tenacity or the energy at seventy years old to still juggle three jobs and three focus groups and other personal development endeavors; it seems to be part of my essential personality.

My parents seemed perfectly comfortable with their efforts. Their minds seemed preoccupied with invisible missions which did not include my wellbeing. My mother mumbled to herself a lot, but I know she was not crazy. It was a survival tactic for her. My father was always walking, singing, praying, or mumbling to himself in a quiet unassuming way. With all of the nonverbal pressure going on within the family and in the world at large, I dismissed any hope of reassuring communication from my parents, siblings, or social advocates. My need for more, better, and different communication became too much, too heavy, and too confusing for me to bear.

I eventually came to understand that I was fearful all the time because my life was dangerous all the time. There was no respite from the horrors; I was surrounded by them. Even the time at home was consumed with unloading, loading, or sorting and resorting enormous piles of stuff poured into our yards. We would unload truckloads of unwanted assorted recycled materials into our backyards every single day, sometimes two or three times a day.

I am not sure when I took notice that there was no longer any space to walk safely to and fro through our backyards. The only place free of junk was the wide alley, which was made of old, discarded – probably recycled – red bricks. Our backyards were not fenced; junk spewed into the edges of the alley. The disorganized, mountains of reclaimed items spilled into the alleyway, leaving our yards looking even more uncivilized. Even so, that's where our three or four large trucks were parked. There were no parking laws for alleys.

After playtime was eliminated, I spoke aloud less and less. When I was about eleven, I noticed with surprise that I felt significant discomfort in the pit of my stomach when I tried to speak. The discomfort increased over time, and I spoke less and less as a result. I cringed when I realized I lacked even such rudimentary life skills as speaking, listening, communicating with others, and advocating for myself.

How would I learn the basic life skills necessary to survival? I understood that I needed to learn to dialogue with others on some simple scale, but I had no idea where to begin. Somewhere along my journey, I had learned that uttering sounds was an indispensable part of living. I understood that sharing conversations was supposed to help me fit in and belong, but for me, trying to communicate with other people only made life worse. No matter how determined I was to practice speaking, I felt more detached from everything and everyone, including myself.

Instead of talking with other people, I would engage in conversations in my own head. I had many characters in my head that would interact with each other, some were regulars, and some were occasional visitors. I can't tell you how many characters were involved, but they kept my mind occupied and I must have at least learned some elementary things about communication from this internal experience. My coping method was not unusual in this respect. My parents didn't talk to each other unless absolutely necessary. In fact, they didn't talk much to anyone at all.

As I observed my parents' limited discussions with one another, I realized, for whatever reason, most of us didn't talk to each other. With twelve siblings now, I could go many days and not share even one conversation was some of them. Even the neighbors learned not to talk face-to-face with my parents; such conversations took place only occasionally, maybe once every blue moon.

Somehow, this absence of verbal communication led me to believe it was okay to be different and not desire the exchange of ideas through speaking. The increasing distress I felt in the pit of my stomach when I was expected to express myself verbally helped me to understand that the non-speaking situation was not normal. I longed to figure out how to improve my language skills within the family.

Chapter 3 - **Spiritually Homeless: 1955-1965**

Waking up to a new sense of personal dignity was a miracle

Just Say No. I could see this age-old dilemma in action as a kid when my parents did not have the power to say *no* when a *yes* was expected, even when saying *yes* would make an already vexing and strenuous situation worse. They regularly agreed to take on more work even when it meant a job would be tripled in time, muscle, and hustle, to undertake yet another vast, unbelievable, and insufferable task.

One of the cruelest add-ons to the already overbearing hauling business was unloading tons of pig-iron and foundry coke from boxcars by hand. The surface of each bar of pig-iron and foundry coke was both rough and jagged; handling these bars was brutal for my little hands. The weight of these bars was far too heavy for me to lift over the side of the gigantic boxcars. We devised a system to pass the bars and chunks assembly-line style, each time passing to the next taller person in line. The person at the end of the line was supposed to throw it into the truck for transporting. The pain from the multiple tiny cuts on each of my fingertips called for nothing short of serious mercy before early morning. While I was wearing a minimum of two pairs of macho gloves, the coarse fabric around the front fingertip area of the gloves would quickly shed away within the first hours of the evening. It was as if someone was using miniature chisels; all protection for my fingertips disappeared many hours before the job was completed. The same thing was true when we worked with the coke. By the end of this process, the fingertips of my gloves were nonexistent because of the harsh, huge, heavy, chunks of black coke. The work was beyond difficult and challenging. I was never sure of the exact weight of the two heavy objects; I just knew the stuff was substantially heavy and abrasive.

I was a little skinny kid. Helping to unload box cars filled with what looked like millions of iron pieces overwhelmed me. Each time we arrived at the foundry to work inside or outside unloading box cars, it took my breath away. Sometimes we'd unload multiple boxcars in one night.

I would climb up into the boxcar, take a deep breath, and then I would begin to pray. It was impossible to wrap my mind around our purpose for being there. This process was nothing short of cruel and unusual punishment, with or without the ruling of a judge or a courtroom. My many tears went unnoticed. The darkness of night came too soon as we labored within the blackness of the boxcars. It was worst during the wintertime; my fingers and toes, and my heart, were all yearning for mercy. Sometimes it was difficult to believe pain could be so quiet and yet so aggressively horrifying. Even though the thin multiple slits on each finger were small and many, each fingertip cried out in pulsating agony. The drama of twenty frozen fingers and toes individually hurting at the same time, screaming for independent attention, was sheer torture. The cruelest part of all was I had to look forward to this season of physical and mental pain every winter for eleven consecutive years.

I am not sure which dimension of the thawing process hurt worse, the slits of torn flesh, the pulsating phase, the tingling stage, or the enormous throbbing sensations at the end of the thawing process. By morning, if I was allowed to attend school, the tips of my fingers, slits and all, were so sore it was impossible to hold my slender yellow number two pencil. The black soot embedded on my skin from handling the large chunks of black coke told a vivid family story. In all of this commotion, I never saw my mother upset, even though her hands must have been cold and frozen too. She rode in the cab of the truck, maybe her hands were rewarmed by the heater.

When my father became a minister, he renovated one of our houses into a storefront church. I was possibly twelve, with four years to go before I would be released from the tribe of tribulations and mayhem. One night while we were praying at our church, we began to hear loud booms, louder than the regular firecrackers I'd heard before. The sounds were unbelievably loud and frightening. The little church shook with each boom. I knew the noises were not normal firecrackers. The noise seemed to continue forever, in evenly timed successions, every three or four seconds. I began to pray more fervently. At this point I pretty much laid my face in my hands. I was not prepared for Jesus or Satan to judge me. I knew I had not yet lived the life I longed to live, a life with order, goals, purpose, and significance.

There were calculated spaces between each loud boom, enough time for me to think maybe the loud, dangerous sounds were over. Nevertheless, there came another and another and many more. The explosions violently shook the walls of our small building. The entrance door of the small sanctuary was open. We were all scared to death. No one moved to close the door or investigate the horrible noise. The extremely loud booms and bangs went on for what seemed like forever. I was so relieved when the sounds stopped.

The next morning, the Kansas City Star printed a story about the new fireworks celebrations at the baseball stadium only six blocks from the church. The stadium officials would have a fireworks display for the winning team's homeruns at the end of the games. The fans at the baseball stadium were enjoying the fireworks, but for us on the outside the sounds were terrifying on the first night.

This was my first experience in learning to distinguish between necessary and unnecessary worry. I had many distressing experiences before and after I turned sixteen. The many different, colorful shapes exploding high in the sky after the games at night were the most exquisite sights I had ever seen. A showcased snapshot of the stadium is all that now stands where the large stadium once stood on Twenty First & Brooklyn Avenue in Kansas City, Missouri.

Our church did not have a large membership. It was our family and three or four visitors. We had an organist for a few years. There was a homeless man, a Seventh Day Adventist, who rented a room at the church for a short period of time. We attended church on Saturdays and Sundays. Occasionally we hosted a large general assembly which was pretty high spirited; guests arrived from a half-dozen neighboring cities, and the little church would be packed to capacity.

I've always participated in church activities from as early as I can remember. Attending church services were pretty much the only social activity within the community where I lived. On Sunday mornings and one other evening during the middle of the week, folks unfailingly attended church services. I would see husbands chauffeuring their wives and children to somebody's church every Sunday. I would see taxicabs arriving like clockwork on Sunday mornings and a couple of nights during the week. I assumed they were going to church because the women wore decorative, wide hats. Their white or colorful churchy-looking attire spoke of their probable destinations. At a very young age it became a burden for me to have a three-way life: go to work, go to church, and go back to work. Later in my life, the church building became a refuge from the fanatical hauling work schedule.

Much later, in my adult life, the church sanctuaries became the only place I could find rest, peace, and sleep. Sometimes, it was the preacher's sermons that appeased my troubled mind and soul, gently allowing me to slumber. Other times, the entire service, from start to finish gave my fatigued spirit a brief timeout. The length of my church naps depended on how exhausted I was from the previous week's demands. I had no idea how to get that kind of relaxed sleep anywhere but on the church pews.

Being very young when I was introduced to the church as a way of life, as a natural occurrence, I was devastated when I learned I had to develop character traits as I grew older. Traits such as determination, patience, tolerance, love, and accountability did not come easily to me. I also grew more fearful and depressed. Anxiety became my new friend and joined forces with my old friend fear. It started in kindergarten and was promoted to the first grade, along with me. When I arrived at second grade, fear was already there, waiting to welcome me. Fear never left my side again from ages six to thirty. No one told me there was a step by step process to obliterate fear or anxiety.

I had heard my father called a reverend, a preacher, a minister, and a man of the cloth; I on the other hand wondered about his exceptional dogmatic dominance over his family in contrast to his given titles. He made sure we had praise and worship daily within the cab of the truck. There was much singing, praying, and reverencing God through reading and quoting scriptures. No one spoke in other tongues or did the holy dance within the family. I was too exhausted to do either. As matter of fact, sometimes I felt that going to hell would be a better trade off than living in hell on earth. The very life of life was missing in our existence. I walked a thin invisible line between belief and disbelief, teeter-tottering back and forth. I was a young, small, innocent, exhausted child. I didn't know what to think or believe, and I didn't know how to figure it out. It seemed just living was a complicated process.

I had an overwhelming feeling that others always wanted to be in my business, managing me, managing my life for me; the truth was I did not have any real business of my own, none at all. After years of being overworked, underfed, not paid, stuffed in the back of a truck, and not allowed to attend school without being completely exhausted, our unsafe, unloved, and unimportant lifestyle grieved my soul greatly. I was disappointed in the process.

I became aware that I needed something in order to be changed, to awaken me, perhaps I was asleep, perhaps I was dreaming. Where could I find the very life of life? In my innocence I was not sure how much of an awakening I needed. However, I was one hundred percent sure that there had to be another way of living, something other than trying to protect myself from the harsh realities of being a young female laborer. There had to be some other way to make a living, something other than trying to protect myself from accidently falling from one of the old, embarrassing, un-sporty trucks. Our work became more unbearable and tedious with each passing day. I was always worried about danger, even though I had never known danger's opposite, safety.

Despite all the hazards, there were still times when – to my young mind – being involved in the hauling business felt like a great trade off. It helped me temporarily forget my fears about school and life. When I was busy kicking boxes, I felt a peace about school. When I was at school, all I wanted was to not be there. I was at my wits end with the hauling business from the second day at age six to the last day at age sixteen. Somewhere along the way I began to feel excessively caged. No matter where I was, I wanted to be somewhere else. I knew the true meaning of being indoctrinated.

The living aspects of my existence were missing in my now twelve-year-old mind and life, but who could I tell, who would believe a child?

I would sometimes ask myself, was my existence on this earth literally to see how much humiliation and abuse I could withstand? Every day it was the same thing: I was awakened morning after morning before dawn, after having stumbled to bed, exhausted, only a few hours earlier. I worked the entire day and on into the scary, midnight hours. Then I would drop into bed, worn beyond exhaustion again. Every day, over and over, this was beyond my understanding. I had no way of knowing if I would still be okay, or even if I would still be alive, at the end of this insane ordeal. This experience was the true definition of trials and tribulations in action for me.

For eleven years, three hundred and sixty-five days each, my life passed in this fashion, without the slightest hint of compassion or thoughtfulness from the people who controlled my every waking moment. The very grownups who were supposed to be keeping me from all hurt, harm, and danger were too wounded to be able to raise their family differently. We were not asked to pick cotton or plow fields, but a view of slavery days often flashed through my mind, nonetheless. If I had known about concentration camps at that time, I would have felt great empathy for the prisoners there. None of the children – the internees – in my family dared to stray an inch beyond the invisible, fixed boundaries of our home front before they reached age sixteen.

I was now losing my childhood willpower. I soon lost the will to care. Mentally everything began to bother me. How would I survive another day, let alone two more years in such tormenting conditions? The business of living was becoming too complex to contemplate surviving. *Only God kept me from losing my mind. I did not know Him, but he knew me.* When I turned sixteen I would be allowed to leave home. I'd watched my six older siblings move into the unfamiliar world and make the best of their lives at sixteen. I thought long and hard, cried, questioned God, prayed, praised, and gave up on learning how to trust God, others, or myself. My parents talked and sang about God being a shelter in the time of a storm. I used to wonder if they knew our lifestyle seemed more like a premeditated blizzard. I had worked with an unbelievable commitment, without an attitude of reproach. I was fresh out of ways to survive my hostile living environment.

My entire life had been one long, relentless, devastating series of storms. I had learned to work without any kind of incentive, to arrive at the pearly gates having never experienced joy, or thanks, or gratitude for a job well done. I wanted a reward for my services rendered from age six to sixteen in my parents' business. I told myself a reward would be given, even though I did not know when. I hoped it would come while I was still on earth rather than waiting until I was in heaven.

I was ready to wait to receive my reward posthumously if that was the will of God. Earlier I had wanted to know what receiving a reward felt like while I was alive. Now I desperately wanted a reward of some kind – any kind, dead or alive. I had counted my blessings as I had seen them right up until I was fifteen years old. At fifteen I stopped in the middle of the kitchen of my home and told this invisible God I was sorry. I could no longer trust that he cared for me on earth or in heaven. I couldn't take it anymore! I had no more energy to trust in a non-caring God. I felt all alone most of the time. I walked out of the back door of the kitchen. I walked around the many huge piles of junk in our backyard. I was now on my own for real. I wanted to be appreciated.

For whatever reason, I let go of the idea of an all loving, caring, and all-knowing Father God. There was a soft sadness within me when I let go. I had so wanted to have someone or something to lean on. My courage and grit continued to evaporate. I could no longer pretend that God or anyone else cared. That was my truth, and I tried to face it. I needed my energy to survive the terrible daily demands. Life became more difficult by the minute. I did not have any time or desire to learn to read, write, or attend school. I often wondered how I would learn the skills necessary to be on my own, to manage my household.

The sadistic workload I faced day, in and day out was too much for a young, unschooled, recycling girl like me. It was very depressing to hear the call every morning. My mother would call from the kitchen "Come on!" in a loud, demeaning, and demanding tone. The kitchen and bedroom were separated by a thin wall. With that command, I would run like a runaway slave child through the dining room, on through the unkempt kitchen, just around the corner and out the back door. Guided only by the humming of the truck motors in the early hours before dawn, I ran toward the tall, raggedy truck waiting in the dark backyard or alley. It was dark outside most of the time in the early morning; even dawn had not awakened yet.

I would run and leap like a gymnast, grabbing hold onto whatever my hands could grasp as I placed one foot inside the rim of the big black truck tire. With my tiny hands I would climb upward into the tall truck bed. If the truck was empty I would climb down into the deserted blackness of the truck bed. Depending on which truck we were using, the truck bed was made of either rough wood or cold steel. If the truck bed was loaded with recycling goods, I would lie upon on whatever material filled the inside of the truck bed. If it was empty, I would adjust and return to sleep on the cold truck floor. God forbid if it was raining. I was always fast asleep in the truck within minutes after essentially sleep running from the humble house to the truck.

I'd gone to bed after midnight the night before, and to turn around and be awakened so early only hours later seemed inhumane, even to my fifteen year old self. That's if it was summer, spring, or autumn. In winter, in the beginning, we kids would be allowed to ride in the cab of the truck. In the end, we rode in the back of the truck no matter the season. It seemed that winter began to represent all of the seasons. In my experience, they were at least metaphorically identical: They were all stony and heartless.

Even though the daily early morning ride to the distribution center was about a forty-five minute drive one way, it always seemed like a five-minute drive because of the lack of sleep. Manipulating all of the recycled material into the truck took much determined energy and skill. What a relief it was to see the gigantic swollen pile of cast-off items shrink twice in a twenty four hour period. It was depressing to know we had to return that night and then the next morning and do it all again.

And always, the one pair of adult male hands remained in the cab of the truck while the females worked thanklessly. The drive home from the distribution company in the mornings seemed to take forever. After fighting the morning traffic back to what we called "the house," it was always eight fifteen or later when we arrived. I would change into something not really fit to wear in public and dash off to school. In the end, I was literally running as fast as my little legs would carry me. I never made it on time, no matter how fast I tried to run, in either elementary or junior high or high school. I was still blocks away when the last bell rang at eight-thirty every morning. I'd speed walk into the classroom as if I did not know what time I was expected to be seated at my desk. I was just relieved to be away from the occupational duties of the family.

Except for the hours I was at school, I would work in the family business from sun up to sun down and then again into the darkest hours of the night, climbing in and out of the back of the old raggedy trucks, emptying various plastic and metal containers. I did this daily from 1953 to 1964. No matter what size the containers were, they all seemed huge to a small female child. It would be 1970 when Stevie Wonder, said it best in his hit song, "Heaven Help Us All."

I felt spiritually and physically homeless. I wanted to wake up to a new sense of personal dignity. I knew without a doubt it would be a miracle if that ever happened. I was torn by the indifference of my parents. Why was my family's lifestyle so demeaning, degrading, and disgraceful? Even if my parents were just minutes away from the reality of their slavery ties, how was I supposed to hold my head up? How was I to walk with any sense of self-worth? These thoughts and more were difficult to dismiss or to own. How, when, or where was I going to learn the skills I needed to be a healthy, functional, adult human being? The idea of ever being able to live as an independent person seemed too farfetched to hope for.

Because I was always working from the time I entered school, I did not have any idea of the many activities a young child like me could or should have experienced. I had to concentrate on aggressively tearing through enormous piles of recycle and manipulating it in countless ways to fit within truck after truck, day after day. There were piles in our backyards, piles to be picked up at the land fields, piles at the distributing company, and piles in and outside of our forty sheds of the companies we serviced.

Sometimes, during the late fifties and early sixties, our parents allowed us to stop work early to attend the late A. A. Allen's tent revival meetings in Kansas City, Missouri. The constant drama of demons sitting in the corners of the tent being mentioned at the services always scared the living crap out of me. "There he is!" the revival preacher would shout. He would then point toward one ceiling corner and then another. He'd point with much drama and charisma. I would look with a jerk and stare, trying to see those fast moving demons the preacher so convincingly seemed to see. It appeared that the creatures he saw always sat high and looked low. I would innocently wonder what their purpose was. If they were demons, why were they looking down at us? The concept did not make sense to me. How could they see us, but we could not see them? Night after night the preacher would see the demons sitting, hopping, and moving about after being freed from some possessed man or woman at the overflowing altar.

I only had so much energy to waste being entertained by yet another suspicious preacher. I believed my parents had wasted enough of my time by preaching one message and living another. As far as I could tell, their messages and actions were totally misaligned.

Nine times out of ten, we would return to work after the service ended at ten or eleven at night. Remembering what awaited me afterward, I lost interest in locating the demons. I had made many sincere attempts at trying to locate the fast-movers. I deemed they were toddler-sized, hideous, mythical creatures. I soon realized they were also far too fast to be caught by my tired eyes. I was already dog-tired, sleepy, and hungry. I gave up trying to see the invisible. Dealing with seeing or not seeing the demons became a risk I would have to take; seeing them was impossible. No matter how I tried, I failed, and soon fell asleep each time.

This entire scene plagued me for many years to come. Much later in life I realized I had been traumatized by the meetings at the old tent revivals. I had an awful time trying to stop myself from questioning whether the preacher had seen what he claimed he'd seen. By now my life was a total mess, and my mind was even messier.

Between the ages of eleven and thirteen, as I worked, I would wonder what the students were doing in the classroom daily. I struggled to understand why my parents did not feel awkward not allowing us to attend school daily during school hours.

Trying to wake up to a new sense of purpose was an ongoing struggle. My sixth grade teacher had once given us an assignment to write a short story and present it in front of the class. As unkempt as I looked and as wounded as I felt, that did not hinder me from presenting. I stepped from my little desk with a blank sheet of notebook paper hiding my face, pretending to read what was not there. I made up the story as I told it. It was a very brief short story, about thirty words including, "Once upon a time. My paper was only to shield me from them. They probably saw and heard a different story rather than the one I presented.

I remember the room was respectfully quiet as I stood telling my story. I stood in front of the not-so-large room, bold and unafraid. That faked reading was my first attempt to participate in a class assignment in seven long years. As I stood that day I was sure the students were surprised to see or hear me speak. I did not stutter or stammer or lose my words. Thinking back, I am not sure the students understood what I had said. I talked extremely low and tremendously fast, without any pauses. Although I'd had some level of satisfaction while reading my make-believe short "Once up on a time" story, by the time I found my way back to my desk I was totally mortified; I wondered what I was thinking. It had taken tremendous courage on my part and the effort did not produce the satisfactory feeling I had hoped for; not even remotely. While my state of affairs bothered me not at all in those standing moments, I was immediately ashamed by my contribution to the class that day. I thought about my need to interact with my peers, I felt awkward. My feelings of unworthiness would increase every time I attempted to think about trying something new and different. My need to participate was greater than my continued focus on my inappropriateness. My unsuitable attire was less than appealing, and that bothered me not in the least. My attendance was unreal: tardy every day, or absent. The horrific hauling and recycling activities at home were beyond description. The harsh, neglectful environment had become the norm. My home was a home of few words, except the words "Shut up" were always loud and plentiful. But somewhere deep down inside of me there was a little nudging instinct that said, "Keep trying, you will win some day."

I usually spoke in fragments, subjects and verbs were not allowed. What I learned that day was I had no reservoir from which to pull stored data. I had not learned anything in the first seven years of attending school. I had failed one class after another. I was not learning anything, even on the few days I was allowed to attend school. I was embarrassed, sleepy, tired, and hungry, and I felt less than wanted, much like the undesirable stuff we hauled for a living.

My junior high school was six or seven blocks farther than the elementary school. I am not sure how many days I attended school in the seventh, eighth, or ninth grades, but I was late every single day. Every day that I did go to school I would spend the entire day trying to stay awake. Between nodding, rocking, and reeling at my desk, sometimes this was the only rest I was able to get. In elementary school, I was always relieved when it was time to go home for lunch even though it only meant I would get some fresh air to wake up for the afternoon session. Once I was back in my seat, though, back to sleep I would go, while staring at the big clock on the right-hand wall of the classrooms between naps.

Going home for lunch in junior high school was not an option. There had not been any food to eat from the time we began working at five in the morning until three-thirty in the afternoon when we returned back home from school.

I am not sure when not attending school at all became my parents' decision for me. During that era, we would get up early every morning just the same and load into the truck. By then it did not matter; I was so far behind in my education that catching up was impossible.

The entire process was difficult to interpret. I could not understand how a kind and loving God, a God as great as the older saints said he was, would allow this to be my reality. As the parents eliminated school from my life, I worked nonstop. As a small child I wanted to play. I was denied playtime. Working became my play. When I grew up, I wanted to act like an adult, but I still had the hunger for play. I began to play house, play dating, play acting grown up, and play God. But, one day life became real and so did I.

My passion for playing had played out. Even so, I still believed there had to be a reward sooner or later. It was past depressing when I finally accepted the reality of what was happening. My keen sense of awareness made the truth more difficult to process. It would have been much easier to act as if I did not know the lifestyle we lived was more abusive than protective. I had a challenging time believing in a Father God or a Mother Mary in years to come. My parents' devotion to the God message left a distance between me and the rulers of heaven. Over the years since then, I've had to learn new and different ways of living, thinking, behaving, and breathing.

Pretty much any and everything human had become almost non-existent in my life. When I was finally dismissed from the family business in 1964, the breath I breathed was the only tool I walked away with. I began the slow process of learning how to take care of myself both mentally and physically. The discomforts of festering heartaches, heartbreaks, and being heartsick were far worse than having far too many of my teeth aching at the same time.

However, my first action was to make my way to the community orthodontics; this appointment was years overdue. I was trying to change the things I could. I wish I could say that a mentor showed up to guide me but that was and is not my story. One reason is I did not trust anyone to get close to me. I was definitely on my own. It was difficult for others to understand my pain, to be more brutally honest it was difficult for me to understand my own pain.

I launched into a search for soul remedies full-time. Next, I purchased bleach creams to clear my baked potato skin and painted on too much 'I Love Lucy' makeup. In the beginning as a young adult, I'd had a difficult time trying to separate my neglected young self from my now responsible adult self. My mind was continuously in conflict with my heart: I knew I needed to get out into the world and gain employment and meet people and learn new things, but my undeveloped social and emotional skills left me wanting to hide from everything and everyone. I was constantly in an inner turmoil, waging battles with myself in an effort to avoid rejection and ridicule. I was trying to accept that my missing values and morals were the way they were going to be forever, and that my assignment was, somehow, to learn to live with the state of my emotional dysfunction as it was. Taking the risk to investigate my downtrodden lack of emotional control seemed useless. My body and mind had taken too many cold-blooded, unforgettable, physical, and mental blows during the unpleasant eleven-year adventure.

I began to wear two or three pairs of Red Fox stockings at the same time, trying to cover my overly scarred legs; another way of changing the things I could change. I wanted to live and be in a different world. Learning to read, write, and become employable became my intense desire. Later I began to call myself the CEO of me; I was the Chief Emotional Officer of my life and decided to take charge of it rather than waiting for the many scars, gashes, and scrapes on my body and soul to heal, mend and blend.

I had dreamed dreams of hope but had never actually lived with hope in reality. The same was true of visions of a better life that had appeared within my dreams; they had never manifested themselves in reality. All I knew was what I was familiar with – dread – for thirty or more years. My many dreams and visions of comfort were impossible to harness and hold onto.

Still, before the dreams of comfort completely faded away, they had, one by one, totally provided me with an anchor of courage to live and not die. Our days always ended just as they began: rushed, unsympathetic, hostile, frustrated, confused, tired, angry, and hungry. Years earlier, there had been food prepared and time to partake of it, but those days were long gone.

My mother had ceased to try to adorn her family as she once had tried. I believe she gave up the first day I was in the kindergarten and little by little as the years went by; by the time I was in the fifth grade my mother had lost the capacity to care about herself or her family's well-being except to work side by side with her husband. She had surrendered.

The message gradually became clearer: I was going to have to fight for every bit of knowledge I could get so I could figure out what human beings needed, and wanted, and how to go about finding what was necessary for me to live a healthier life.

One treacherous winter in the Midwest, three of us girls plus our male gatekeeper were shoveling what looked like at least five feet of snow from the sidewalk in front of our home. A stranger walking by stopped and asked, "Are you all boys?" All three of us girls said in unison, "Yes, sir." Our gatekeeper spoke up and said, "No, sir, they're not boys." That was the first and last time I ever heard our male gatekeeper speak up in our defense.

It was difficult to understand what the man had asked us. The ice cold snow was whirling and hissing around our faces. It was impossible to think about our gender. We just responded to the man's question automatically, "Yes, sir" (be polite, don't argue). Our job was to do as we were told, regardless of the weather. If I had died while outside shoveling snow in a blizzard, I don't know if my parents would have been much bothered. The weather, both summer and winter, was cruel in the Midwest. My parents were unmoved by Mother Nature's destructive force, as long as we kept working.

As I shoveled the snow from our walkway, the blowing wind and snow created a thin blanket of snow on my face. My mind was on the lack of heat inside of the house when we were finished. My only motive for wanting to attend school was to avoid the recycling business. I learned to live with persecution either way, at home and school. I never received any recognition as a great worker, but it would have made no difference. I knew I was a great worker, and that knowledge gave me some kind of kid power I could not explain.

Still, the untraditional lifestyle depressed me greatly and left me with only a vague interest in school. I wasn't learning anything there anyway, and I learned pretty quickly that it couldn't protect me from the recycling business. In my culture, most of us did not find the tools for life and living in our community circles – not at school, or at church, or from friends or neighbors. When it came down to it, we usually had to choose the lesser of the unclear, unpleasant, and difficult mountains placed in front of us. Other, easier options were simply unavailable.

Much later in life I embraced one of the most empowering ideas known to mankind. That idea is this: "I have a choice." The realization came late, but it came.

While there had been food, warmth, and a feeling of home-sweet-home once upon a time, kind and loving communication was always absent.

There were many demands spoken. "Hurry up." "Move," "Who took this or that?" "Did you hear me?" "Come on!" "Get out of my way!" And, "you, come here!" "Oh, it's you." "You," was used so much instead of my name – "Leona" – that learning to respond to my name was a slow and awkward process. One day seemed like a long time to me then, as a small child. One week seemed like an eternity.

Time passed by so slowly as one unpleasant event occurred after another. I must admit, the first day in the family business was not difficult at all. The thousands of days that followed were most difficult, even after I accepted the reality that it was going to be a very long "season of winters." At a very young age I noticed my older sibling either being put out of the house for one reason or another by my father or at sixteen or they got married. Therefore, I just assumed sixteen was the cut off time for staying in the family home.

At sixteen I was dismissed physically from the hauling business. It was mid-1964. I was greatly disturbed, confused, and frustrated about who I was and who I was not. I tried to continue attending high school after I was released from the family business. It did not go well. I was too far behind, with no hope of catching up. Before too long, I chose to drop out. The choice was not too difficult. My inner demons and insecurities were egging me on as I walked to my school locker that day to remove my belongings. The last straw had been my inability to decipher one of Helen Keller's poems in my literature class. I didn't know how to do what was required, and I didn't know what the process was to learn how.

Chapter 4 - **Unexpected Stages of Grace**

Bread of heaven, bread of heaven, feed me until I want no more!
~William Williams

The same week I was released from our family hauling business, I made a conscious decision to attempt to show up on time for school, five days a week. I wanted to catch up my grades and move on to the tenth grade. I had repeated the ninth grade three consecutive times, because I had been missing in action from school so much of the time. I had not the motivation to study during the twelve years; but I had a yearning to be present, to learn, to forget about the past. I found it impossible to successfully comprehend the curriculum even when I gave it my best effort. After a week or so, I dropped out of high school. As I walked away slowly, I felt that I was leaving something behind that I desperately needed, but I was still puzzled as to what I was already missing.

I'd moved upstairs from one of the three small overcrowded bedrooms downstairs. Upstairs were four rooms: a large living room, a dining room, a bedroom, and a kitchen. At first, I occupied the entire upstairs. I sensed a deep, intense uneasiness in every room. I finally settled for using only the living room upstairs as a kitchenette. All of the exceptionally large four large rooms upstairs felt eerie to me; I was not sure why.

I was still filled with inexpressible, terrifying fears, and felt I was dying for a drink of "living water." I had no idea what the words "Living Water" referred too. The saints I'd known were not able to communicate or discuss their sacred spiritual experiences. I had heard and read countless scriptures time and time again, but I was not enlightened with any divine interpretation.

My father had built two additional rooms adjacent to the single bedroom downstairs for us kids. I slept in each room at some point, and the next thing I knew, I was sleeping upstairs, just like that.

I felt uneasy sleeping in one of the large middle rooms upstairs. It had a full-size bed near a spooky back porch window. There was something about the room and the window that troubled and frightened me daily. Clutter, junk, and unwanted items stared back at me from the screened-in back porch window next to the bed in the middle. I never understood my edgy disposition while I tried to sleep in this particular room. Still, I had some space and maybe some privacy, something I had never had before.

My parents decided I should enroll in beauty school. I had grown accustomed to my non-communicative environment at home. Once enrolled in the Arlene Jefferson School of Beauty in 1964, I struggled in many social areas. Being a student and interacting with the other students was most challenging. It was also perplexing to honor the instructors at the academy.

Once my parents had paid my enrollment fee, I found a job to pay my tuition myself. I was now a fulltime student, fulltime employee, and a fulltime-partier. Once I completed the beauty school course, I worked a while longer and lo and behold I found myself pregnant. I resigned from the job. The baby was still born. I stayed in the hospital for seven days. When I was finally released my grief was overwhelming. I was not prepared for the turmoil that followed. Even though the baby was unplanned, the loss was tremendous and I was troubled.

Losing my child was all I now had to show for the nine-month experience. It became difficult to sleep during the night after having seen death so close back at the hospital. It was even more difficult having no one, absolutely no one, to talk to about the great loss of my baby and my non-existent sense of self. The communication factor remained missing within the family. My folks went on with their lives and business as usual. I wished I had someone to confide in about the death and dying ordeal that had just taken place.

One day maybe a week or so after I had been released from the hospital I had drifted off to sleep in the dingy middle bedroom upstairs. I woke up suddenly, sat straight up, and proceeded to swing my legs off the left side of the extra-high bed. The bed was so high I should have had a stepstool to climb from the bed. With my elbow resting on the mattress, I tried to push my 120-pound body from the bed to a standing position. Something was wrong. The simple, normal process of getting in and out of bed was not working. I realized I was without any sensation in my lower extremities. Missing the response in my legs and feet for even a small moment was devastating. Astonished, I began to focus on how to fall to the floor and keep moving forward at the same time.

After literally tumbling to the floor I begin scrambling forward toward the living room entrance, straight ahead. My new hindrance had my complete attention. I had to use my upper body to pull my numb legs along behind me. I kept using my arms to drag myself forward.

Somehow, despite my bewilderment, I kept dragging my useless legs until I was halfway into the living room. I saw nothing but the large, inviting, living room window. I moved across the floor as quickly as I could, grateful that I could move at all. I finally made it all the way to the window. This spot became my place of comfort for the next few days. I continued to lean on the window sill on into the night, watching the many stars and then the few cars, listening to Aretha sing on the record player and waiting for day light. Sitting by the window gave me some semblance of peace. The night darkness and fresh air spoke to me and spooked me at the same time.

Many different unpleasant scenes from my stay at the hospital came back to me repeatedly. One scene particularly was when I awoke from being sedated, a nurse was standing by my hospital bed holding a bundle I assumed was my baby. "Is that my baby?"

"Yes," she said, "but he's dead."

Surely there must have been a better way to announce such a tragedy.

I was terrified of having to return to that the merciless hospital. I sat by the window all night. I was afraid to go back to sleep.

Eventually, comforting messages began to come to me as I sat by the window, "It's going to be all right."

"Yeah, right," I would say right back to it.

"What am I going to do?" I'd ask myself.

Answers never came about what I should do. Gradually, though, the feeling returned to my lower limbs and I was ultimately able to regain control over them. I welcomed the overwhelming relief when my health was back to normal. I dared not move for a long time for fear the condition would return.

Looking out the large window, it almost seemed that I was seeing Brooklyn Street for the first time. I felt the feeling of being home at last, briefly.

My family lived downstairs. No one ever came upstairs to visit or check on me, not a soul. I prayed that I would recover and sort out my life. I was grateful just to feel better! This was another "small moment with a great meaning." As frightening as those few moments or seconds were, even more disquieting was the fact that there was no one to cry out to for help. Before and during the pregnancy I was treated like an outcast; however, after the pregnancy season was over I was somehow treated even worse. My parents had always ignored me. I did not know there was room for worse treatment from them, but their refusal to even acknowledge my existence was worse.

Ernest Hemingway wrote about a "clean, well-lighted place." That upstairs living room, with its comforting window, became my healthy, well-lit place, for a brief time.

When I was strong enough to revisit those few weeks, the devastation had been far worse than I wanted to recall. It took many years for me to be able to face all that had happened and the unnerving consequences that were a part of the grieving process.

I had learned how to pretend; pretending kept me alive while I became strong enough to face my truth without further psychological damage. My unpleasant childhood had left me plum numb, with a feeling of unworthiness and indifference. My attitude became "it was what it was." I convinced myself it didn't matter. On the other hand, I developed a powerful resentment toward my parents, and toward my own vulnerabilities. I was not sure why I had such a hard time forgiving my parents or myself, but I couldn't seem to find the grace in my heart to start the forgiveness process.

As soon as I walked up the winding steps that led to my room, I would sit by the window. The bottom of the window was about two feet from the floor. I could comfortably lean on the windowsill as I sat on the floor. Watching the bumper-to-bumper, slow-moving traffic, thinking and wondering, I wondered what made life come alive for others while I felt oh so empty.

I decided to move all of my belongings to the living room and abandon the other three rooms upstairs. I grew stronger each day and moved a little more of my meager belongings until nothing was left in the other three rooms. Now I resided solely in the upstairs large living room.

I would sit looking out through the living room window all night until daybreak, and then just before dawn I felt safe enough to fall asleep on a pallet I had made on the floor. I felt safe listening to Aretha Franklin singing, "God will take care of you!" In some small way I had to trust her message was true for others, but not for me. I was still trapped in my grief. I had depended on my vigils at the window to help me process the steady stream of complicated feelings and memories. I discovered I was suspicions, anxious, insecure, immature, and constantly afraid of everything and everybody. I had given the feeling of failure a new definition…doomed. Looking back at it now, I can safely say I was in my first tentative stages of figuring out who I was and trying to get to know myself better. I was in limbo, I didn't know myself at all, and the numbness of my emotions was scary and uncomfortable.

Learning how to accept myself for who I was, appreciating my strong points and owning my weaker ones, was even more petrifying. "What would happen if I did not like myself as I was, or who I thought I was predestined to become?" I could not conceive of loving myself. I certainly did not understand the need for loving others.

Even after my life moved on, I remained deeply pre-occupied with trying to make sense of my existence. I was without even the smallest physical appetite for food during my teens and twenties. I was forced to remember to eat every three days by way of an acute painful headache. My nothingness of a future had me completely bewildered.

I wanted to run away from me. I wondered how many years it would take for me to stand and face my reality. At first, I ran from one encounter to another, time after time. I was reminded of a documentary I once watched: "Running from Crazy." My lack of education was starting to cost me more time and energy than I was willing to accept. I now knew what I had left behind when I walked away from the high school a few years earlier. I needed to learn to how to think, behave, and live differently. And, I needed to figure out why I was always so edgy; I learned it wasn't the window at all that made me edgy, it was life.

I had experienced so much loss, and I had zero emotional or intellectual resources to fall back on or to use as coping mechanisms. I had to discover reasons to want to live. I wanted nothing more than to be healed from my horrible state of affairs, but I had no idea where or how to begin the healing experience.

Hope had been snatched from my timid grasp over and over again. The only safe sources and resources of comfort were the flickering stars zillions of miles away, high in the sky. I watched from my window at night, hoping, trying to forget what nine months and death had somehow slipped in and taken from me, just a week before. At that young innocent age, I had not been rocketed into a spiritual place. I was in a place where only daylight felt and seemed safe in some small way; and, nightfall, night hours, felt and seemed unsafe, like death and danger in some large way.

I was now nineteen years old and I had no more idea what I was going to do with my life than I had at six years old. I would continually ask myself: "What am I going to do?" "Why did my experiences with loss and losing seem so great?" "Why did my experiences with winning seem so rare and unlikely?" "How can I change these patterns so I lose less and win more?" "What is happening within me and around me?" I continuously asked and wondered and found no answers.

I felt immobilized by my inability to assess my situation and make decisions about how to move forward. I didn't know where or how to start the recovery process. I had more questions I couldn't answer: "When would my sense of life and living emerge into a more purposeful meaning?" "How or when would I stop feeling so painfully shy, battered, and misused?" "Did I deserve any benevolence?" Sitting by the window, tentative thoughts tried to suggest that I was on my own with this desire to support myself in my movement into health, wholeness, and peace. I had no idea how to support my ambition to attract health, self-fulfillment, or joy. Yet, there was this thought which lingered around in my head nonstop: "Suppose no one shows up to rescue or assist you from this twisted, uncomfortable, mental prison of gloom and doom?" The thought of solving my own problems of loneliness, and rejection, and addressing my undeniable feelings of displacement, was perplexing. These and more emotions were so overpowering that I could not begin to contemplate controlling the emptiness or letting go of the self-manufacturing craziness. What would I do if I could find no one to help me? The unwelcome thought of becoming an independent self-advocate for mental, emotional, physical, and spiritual self- healing whirled around and around in my head. My case seemed impossible.

In 1966, the civil rights movement was chaotic and scary. Some bus drivers had their own attitudes concerning the social changes that were and were not needed. I only rode the bus when absolutely necessary. My understanding of the civil rights movement was not clear; I was more concerned with being employed long term in order to have bus fare. It was not long before I purchased my own transportation. Having my own vehicle broadened my ability to go where I wanted to go, when I wanted to go, which in turn unleashed a desire to escape faster, and quicker. Having the ability to leave when I needed to eventually tamed my pent-up need to always be somewhere else.

The mental gremlins continued to push and pull me into the depths of self-pity. They also mocked my efforts to become my own advocate. My sarcastic subconscious thoughts mimicked and ridiculed me endlessly. The idea to investigate or question my belief system or my behavior slipped away again and again. I couldn't hold on to productive behaviors or thoughts, even when I recognized their potential to change my life; Try as I might, I couldn't seem to shake the sense of conspicuous unacceptability that had accompanied me most of my life. I clearly remember the badge of dishonor that attached itself to me the day my parents drove one of the large raggedy business trucks right up in front of my elementary school where everyone could see it. I didn't know what to do! I was a third grader at the time. Should I climb down from the bed of the embarrassingly huge truck or should I remain hidden? My parents were waiting for me to climb down, as they sat in front of the truck. I didn't want anyone at the school to see me and associate me with the truck or the business it was tied to. Finally, I climbed down. That was the day I realized there was such an emotion as shame. I also realized much later in life that there is a thin line between public shame and private ignorance. That day in third grade, I had hoped so desperately that no one had seen me. Years later, I realized my shame came because I had finally seen the situation as it was, and I had faced me.

This experience was one of many childhood wrongs I had to find a way to make peace with in my own heart. The memory of that third-grade decision to get off the truck where people could see me and associate me with the family hauling business permanently occupied a front row seat in my mind. For years to come I did not know how to cope with my shameful experiences that were not of my own making. Did not my parents know the depth of my mortification, degradation, and embarrassment or was I the only one who was bothered by these unkind, uncouth, and downright intolerant events?

I remember needing and wanting to laugh and be excited as a young teenager. I remember how difficult it was to want to openly laugh and have fun, only to realize there was very little about my life that brought pleasure. I wanted nothing more than to be removed from my environment, but how?

The best way I can describe my childhood life is to say it was kind of like watching relentless reruns. I never knew which rerun was going to replay itself in my mind or which clip would routinely pause or which rerun would become a weekly series. I could not follow the confusing procession of chaotic scenes that paraded around in my head morning, noon, and night from six to sixteen years old and then from sixteen to thirty.

I typically lived in the past; I didn't understand present solutions or ways of thinking, it seemed. Past drama dictated the course of each current day. Maturity was hard to come by within the family. I was starved for all forms of nourishment: mental, spiritual, and physical. I was fiercely angry about nothing in particular, just everything. I was immobilized by both known and unknown situations.

Most nights upstairs, I listened to Aretha Franklin sing, "God Will Take Care of You." I would ask myself, "How or when is he going to start taking care of me?" Aretha would sing the lyrics, "He will take care, He will take care of you," over and over. Although, I believed her, I just did not believe this God she was singing about could take care of my grossly neglected self or help to heal my heart from all the abuse. I knew I would have to do my part, but I could not figure out what my part was. With all of my fears so prevalent, my own life was mayhem and my own ability to understand what was happening was limited. "Just what is my part?" I asked myself this question many times.

In the mornings, I had watched the cars going north to get on the Lewis and the Clark viaduct headed for work from my window. In the evening I would watch the north-bound cars from earlier now headed south-bound. Watching the cars move helped me to imagine myself taking action in my own life. The constant routine somehow freed me from my emotional paralysis temporarily. I was always trying to figure out how to live outside of my world. It never occurred to me to try to make changes starting with where I was and envisioning where I wanted to go. I began to sing "Father I stretch my body, mind, and soul to thee!"

Chapter 5 - **Examined Stages of Growth:**

1966

Early September 1966. I walked slowly up the nine or ten winding steps. The Midwest weather had been exceptionally hot and humid that day. I was exhausted, returning from only God knew where, baffled by my mess of a life. I still don't know how many different restless mental processes dictated my daily actions and thoughts. My thoughts and actions were seldom congruent, but on this particular day everything seemed aligned, even in my confusion of the moment. My focus was on one thing only: getting some rest. The very thought of being able to stop for rest gave me comfort.

I was weary, even at the relatively young age of nineteen. It had been a little over three years since my dismissal from the family business. The eleven year pent-up frustration was driving me crazy. I had naively believed escaping the physical part of the family business would make me feel better; however, I felt worse. I was both sadly mistaken and disappointed. I had waited for so long for the day I would be released from the environment, body, mind, and soul. What I didn't know was it wasn't just the work I needed to be released from. As I climbed the winding stairs a palpable twinge of discomfort and foreboding climbed with me.

The only time I ever received any relief was when I was able to sleep; sleep took me away from the stress and strain of my past, my present, and my blurry future. When I opened my eyes each day, my frustration was always waiting for me. Guilt, shame, and grief from my present and past would overtake me without warning as soon as my eyes opened. Over time, even going to sleep was no help. It did not bring peace as it once had done. Instead, flashbacks and visions raced wildly in and out of my mind during all hours, whether I was awake or asleep. Chaotic thoughts traveled through my head relentlessly, at lightning speed. I lost hope. I didn't believe I could ever get past my many emotional challenges.

On this day, all I wanted to do was enter my room and lie down. This feeling, lying down, was the first rewarding sensation I could ever remember desiring so badly. Just anticipating rest seemed heavenly. The anticipation of entering my room and lying down on my pallet dominated me both physically and mentally.

When I finally turned at the bend of the long staircase, what I faced was more than ghastly. I was already fatigued, and the sight that greeted me left me speechless. As I fully digested what my senses were telling me, I simultaneously became aware of an astonishing truth again. I could not see any kind of a decent future for myself through the past abuse and the present abuse. What I did see, though, separated me from the familiar tortures of the life I had become accustomed too. I'd heard the words "Release Me," softly, from within my head and my heart, and just hearing the two words was both freeing and frightening. I immediately felt released from who I had been, what I had been, and where I had been! But the thought of finding a new pathway terrified me. I knew I had much to learn. I was happy to be set free from the shackles others had placed upon me. I wanted to be released from the God my parents were so determined to submit to. I wanted to be released from the timid, oppressed, frightened creature that was me. For a very brief moment, I was free. The grueling mental prison I had learned to accept as comfort was no more, for about one second.

"When will these living nightmares end?" I shouted to no one in particular. My entire life up to that point had been riddled with insurmountable difficulties. My trial-and-error existence was deeply unbalanced. I was sick and tired of life as I had known it. I was confused and baffled.

Someone had been hard at work in my absence. I stood staring blankly at what my eyes were witnessing. Two crisscrossed two-by-fours had been affixed across the outer doorframe of my upstairs entrance. It blocked my access to the room upstairs. The symbolism of this unexpected new sight was too horrifying to internalize. It may as well have been screaming loudly "Do Not Enter!" The crisscrossed boards seemed more like stern guards. One solitary nail pierced the middle of the perfectly made "X." All five gleaming metallic nail tops glowed brightly against the new caramel-stained wood. Whoever had chosen to act rather than speak had made their point unquestionably clear. Yes, they had shut me out just like that, whoever the culprits were. I had been shut out without warning, banished, no "have a nice life," no nothing from that day to this.

I was too exhausted to care. This harsh and relentless cruelty had to be stopped. It had gone on far too long, since I was six to be exact, and now I was nineteen. This was my first step toward living. I was not in the mood for another vivid *Dragnet* or *Perry Mason* suspense rerun. I had noticed conflicts within the family were handled in one of two ways, by prayer or by ignoring it. I instantly chose the latter, for the moment.

The symbolic message spoke like thunder: "Get out!" Yet there was not a soul around, and not a sound had been made. The silent, obscure communicators had not failed at their intended purpose. I felt no urge to twist the doorknob or ring the doorbell. My intuition told me to leave. I obeyed. The madness had won. I affirmed the unspoken request and vacated the premises. I'd heard the old folks imply that difficult moments could be solved with prayer. They had even professed that prayers covered a multitude of wickedness and blatant offenses. This, however, was not my verdict. I somehow knew all of my little prayers tallied less than zero. Nothing persuaded me to bargain or plead with God at all this time. I had silently prayed and pleaded to my parents' invisible God for my entire life. Now I was tired of the nothingness I had been getting in return.

I turned and headed back down the stairs. My physical and mental fatigue disappeared like magic. Now I was hurt, and angry, and energized. Once I reached the bottom of the stairs, I marched diagonally across the large, unkempt downstairs living room and stepped out the front door onto the screened-in porch. A short concrete walkway led to the last half dozen red brick steps leading down to the sidewalk. I never looked back.

Where am I supposed to go after such savage eviction? I staggered up Brooklyn Avenue in a state of shock. I walked as if I knew where I was going. I was headed toward Eighteenth Street. It was my final exit from only the second house I had ever called home.

That top-of-the-stairs moment of despair and awakening was not new; it was just a different version of the past many years of abuse from my parents. I'd had my share of gross, painful experiences at their hands; that day was the final insult. I walked until I calmed down, and then I decided to visit my oldest sister, who lived on Twenty-Ninth Street.

The scorching Midwest summer heat enveloped me unmercifully and made me even more miserable. I slowly walked the thirteen-block trip, which took longer than usual. By the time I arrived at my sister's place, a wall of protection had built itself around the blocked entrance door experience and my internal reaction to it. My deeply offended and hurt spirit was somehow covered until a better day arrived. I did not utter a word to my sister about the eviction experience; my mind and my heart had isolated it and stuffed it away where it couldn't hurt me anymore. Somehow, I was able to pretend the eviction trauma never happened: it had totally disappeared from my mind. I could not envision it nor feel the discomfort it had caused just minutes before. Somehow, the harsh reality had blocked its ugliness.

I was physically and mentally traumatized to the point that, even an hour or so later I felt absolutely nothing and for the next six or seven years. Looking back, all I can say is "what a difference a good walk made that day. I was not upset as far as I could tell. The scene had clumsily intermixed with my many other chaotic, sadistic, childhood accidents and incidents. Everything I owned had been stolen from me and kept from me on the other side of that blocked door in my parents' house. Years later, I wondered if I had been a coward to not request or demand my belongings. I didn't know! At the time, my deep-seated feelings of nothingness signaled that I had no right to life, let alone anything else.

Before the lockout, I had been employed steadily for one year, for the first and last time over the next decade. I worked on and off during those ten years but could not remain on any one job for any meaningful length of time. I had a very limited attention span, which made it difficult for me to be accountable or responsible. Keeping long-term employment was more challenging than I could manage. Something in my emotional make-up kept me from holding steady employment. I had instead many short-term employers who would tolerate my errant behavior until I panicked and ran away again.

I was running out of hope and rope. I had begun to drink alcohol at seventeen. What I noticed was no matter how much alcohol I consumed I could not rid myself of the mental and physical devastations of my youth.

Grief and never-ending childhood cruelty simply left me without enough energy to analyze the many hurts I had suffered, or to learn better ways to cope with my rejections and my resentment. Whenever I thought about the eviction trauma at all, I invariably concluded that it had surely taken more time to conjure up the nailing plot than it would have taken for them to be civilized and talk with each other.

I felt then that it was not difficult to walk away; it was almost a relief. I suppose this was because of my emotional numbness. I just couldn't let myself process the possible motives behind my being forbidden to enter; I couldn't see a significant meaning. Over time I've come to understand that my parents were doing the best they knew at the time.

I never retrieved any of my possessions. I never missed the items that were left behind that nailed-shut door. I do remember feeling as if I were a character in an impromptu performance. I wanted to know the plot, but no one could tell me the story, nor would they tell me what my role was supposed to be. I was making an exit from a segment of the drama where I knew the irrational back story much too well. Some chapters seemed to be missing – perhaps they had been torn out of the script.

I could not imagine what the next scene would be, or who the other characters would be, or how the story would proceed from where my character exited the scene. I felt as if I had missed rehearsal for the last act of play. I simply wanted to run off the stage of life and forget I was ever born. I looked for an end for that story for many years.

I planted my thin-soled shoes on the scorching hot sidewalk that day, and I headed south. The blazing sun embraced my face with each step I took. I wondered if the eviction was the beginning or end of my story. Still, as I was walking away, I wondered – I hoped - I was walking into the beginning of a new story. I also sincerely hoped I was leaving the worst scenes of tragedy behind me. At the time, I didn't have the language to describe the hell I experienced that day, let alone the other nineteen years of living hell. I wanted to say good-bye to ignorance, but ignorance kept saying hello!

While fleeing from the barricaded door at the top of the stairs, a faint thought of marriage as a survival option entered my already troubled mind. This idea was all I could muster in response to this latest physical and emotional upheaval. A small thought suggested who I was to marry. These new ideas were confusing, but no other options or solutions revealed themselves to my fragmented brain.

The thought of marriage made me swallow extra-hard and take a couple of deep breaths. I had a name in my head, but I didn't know the young man well at all. I had met him possibly as many as ten years earlier in a youth ministry class. Nevertheless, three months later I was a married young woman. By December 1966, the matrimonial ritual idea had won. As I think about it now, I am surprised by my resourcefulness. Even in a time of life altering calamity, I found a way to keep fighting for survival. It wasn't perfect, but the arrangement served a purpose.

I desperately needed to be forgiven for my responses to the turn of events in my life. I had never had control over what happened to me – I knew that. Thus far, all I had known of life was neglect, grief, and deviousness. It seemed to me, though, that my reactions weren't what they should've been. I couldn't be certain of my actions or my motives. I felt that all the choices I had made under duress generally didn't serve me well in the long run. It seemed to me that I had always acted compulsively, without thinking. I had been exposed to too much unkindness, cold heartedness, and revulsion. I had been enmeshed in other people's unwanted leftovers as a way of life. In a way, I came away from the locked out experience feeling like I was bad news winnowed out from yesterday's insignificant news. These feelings did not leave any room for sane behavior, dazzling expectations, or noble beliefs. My leap-first-and-look-later survival philosophy was yielding poor results in my life's journey. This process of always having messes to clean up hijacked a large portion of my time, time that would have been better spent getting my life in order.

Something, somewhere, had given me the idea that I had to be exonerated by someone other than myself. It was probably tied to the religious teachings I had heard at church about grace, sin, and redemption. Whatever it was, unfortunately, I found the forgiveness process fiercely irritating. Although, I had not chosen the family business as my way of life, I had to forgive my parents just the same. I knew forgiving them was the first step toward preparing to forgive myself when the time was right. Who could fault my parents for at least trying to raise their family the best way they knew how, even if it included a wickedly twisted sense of dignity?

The family business lifestyle had stolen from me every ounce of self-respect before any sense of self or seeds of dignity had ever begun to germinate for me. The self-respect and unconditional love so essential to nurturing a young child to maturity were either corrupted or misplaced. As a child, I had known that I wanted to flower and grow into a promising healthy young adult. I never had that opportunity. I finally learned much later that real growth meant facing life's music, no matter how low or high, intense or sweet, shrill or calm, and finding solutions to problems from the environment around me and from lessons learned from my prior experiences. Somewhere along my way, I had become aware that repeated failures could sometimes prepare one for repeated successes, especially when the results of failed efforts were used as learning growth opportunities. This phase of cognitive awareness and growth brought much commentary from my colleagues and relatives. Learning to shield myself from criticism (both invited and volunteer) has been possibly one of the most staggering challenges I've had to learn to work through. As a young adult and a newly married woman, I was beginning to learn the rhythm of moving in and out of different growth stages of life, whether those steps and stages were obvious or just part of the experience.

Chapter 6 - **Closed-Minded Living: 1967**

The abrupt dismissal from my family home also meant the only life I had ever known was over. A part of me welcomed the freedom of not being duty bound to work with my parents any longer; another part of me felt lost without working in the mismanaged family business. I had endured silent scorn as I worked side by side with my parents since I was six. And now at nineteen years old I was being released again to endure my new season of grief alone. My parents had served me with an eviction notice created by using two pieces of wood and five spike nails.

I begin to face many looks of disgust from others in my new world. How would I start to rebuild my broken life? Although I was terrified by having been barred from my room and forced to leave without any verbal explanation or my personal belongings, some small sense of hope had begun to dance around in my mind. Sitting by the window had added moments of comfort to my life, yet I felt bored to death. The urgent need to relocate to another place of comfort was most uncomfortable. My search was on to make peace with my emptiness, sorrow, and grief. I wondered how I would learn the process of developing greater self-worth.

I was still trying to get to know the value of life and living when the abrupt midafternoon 2x4 banishment came and simply deepened my feelings of uselessness, helplessness, and inadequacy. Finding a way or a reason to begin my quest for a better life was not easy. I searched day and night, even in my dreams, for a way to reconstruct my worn out mind. The harder I searched, the more deserted and desperate I felt. Inch by inch bitterness was secretly robbing my soul and overtly brutalizing my spirit moment by moment. As I had approached the top of the stairs to try to make peace with the grief of losing my child just a few days prior to August 11, 1966, I faced yet another unanticipated, despicable, soulless act from one or both of my gatekeepers. I was fed up. I was ensnared by a sense of indecency, unworthiness, and self-pity. I knew I had been treated unfairly, but I was not equipped to put up any resistance against such destructive physical and emotional attacks. I had not learned how to protect myself from the wrath of others. I had not acquired a healthy belief system. I was not able to articulate what I felt in words. I could not sleep at night at all, I did not have an appetite, I was sadder than sad, and I worried about my past nonstop. What kept me from going totally crazy upstairs was listening to Aretha Franklin's voice and the music. I valued listening to Aretha Franklin's music, which had been my only form of entertainment upstairs. She was my first champion. Listening to her music was like a refuge, like a support system.

Everything was a challenge for me. Even seemingly small tasks were daunting: things like having all the utilities paid at the same time, or learning how to shop for groceries, or figuring out how to act so I would feel welcomed in my own skin. I discovered certain normal life necessities, which increased my value; like flipping on a light switch and knowing there would be light simply because I had paid the bill. While facing new internal challenges like trying to stop my inner pain, I began to wish for the end. The lack of hope for controlling my emotions was frightening to me. I had been hungry, angry, and lonely and tired all at the same time for many years. I found great rewards in having and exercising my new freedoms, although it was often one traumatic experience after another, especially in the beginning. I was now twenty years old. I was late in learning essential housekeeping and living skills and it was difficult to want to learn to cook when I lacked a steady appetite. I found second-hand furniture to arrange and rearrange daily in my small duplex. I toyed briefly with the idea of learning to read and write. I wished I had an interest in something other than excessive worrying, blaming and, job bouncing. Since I didn't know what else to do I'd arrange and rearranged my furniture every single day to pacify my overpowering need to stay busy. Early in childhood, I had lost any sense of value as a human being, if it had ever been there at all. I wanted desperately to find my sense of self somehow

Household experiences were new and different for me, even paying bills. I did not want to purchase anything on credit. I reasoned I would be duty bound to work forever. I fought to pay up front for everything I acquired after I left home. I did not want a lot of debt obligating me to work a nine-to-five job, especially since I was having a difficult time staying on a job.

I did want to be employed, but found I was a bona fide job hopper, staying only two or three weeks per job, some days a week or a day or so. Filling out applications gave me a lot of practice on my writing skills. I found after a time that having to search for new work every couple of weeks was distressing, but again it kept me busy. The acceptance of my own struggle was difficult. I wanted desperately to maintain employment and worked and worked to overcome my challenges with it.

My husband was another refuge for me and my ongoing, continual issues of life. My issues were many, though, and being married held my pain and contempt at bay for only a brief while. I had not believed I could live beyond my pain and deep shame of my past. The man I married was a man of few words or wishes. I had mistaken his modest personality for the absence of hopes or dreams. By contrast, I had far too much hyperactive commotion always going on, which I had mistaken for ambition. And I did not have any idea how to start life in a space with another human being.

I remembered attending my husband's grandfather's church when I was much younger; our social life had been in association with the church and public school. Most families back then seemed to assume sitting in church led to becoming a mature self later. I've since learned that evolving into a whole human being is greatly influenced by more than where one might choose to sit, in church or otherwise. I saw the world through unhealthy blinders as a child. I worried if there was enough time in life to address all of my grosser deficiencies. There had been little teaching about healthy living in my early home environment. There had been even less healthy learning at church, one place where I'd spent a lot of time.

I pondered whether the rules of life for desperate people were different from the rules for healthy people. I needed to find the energy, strength, and will to fight the undertow of despair, and some incentive to sustain life itself. The desire to rise above my impoverished beginnings drove me forward, but how to accomplish this was a challenge beyond my limited understanding.

What I knew for sure was that tools for healthy development were definitely missing from my still inadequate skill set.

I was on a mission to learn how to tolerate, appreciate, and finally love myself. I thought about the authentic "me" very seldom, simply because I was not in tune with the counterfeit me. I had not a clue who I could become; I did not know who I was.

Unlike my husband at the time, I wanted to be accepted as being someone I did not believe I could ever become. I tried to make myself believe that living a life of role-playing was my only choice. I tried pretending to be happy. I tried pretending that forgiving was not essential. I tried pretending that having genuine self-worth was unnecessary. I tried pretending to accept bogus forms of love. And I tried rationalizing that real learning and change were possible for others, but not for me. Ultimately my broken spirit assigned me a script I could neither live with nor live without. Somewhere I read, "Emotionally healthy people can enhance their dreams of real contentment and joy." I pondered this concept, but it was too far out of reach. I knew nothing about contentment or joy, let alone where to begin to become emotionally healthy.

I had hoped that the marriage would make me feel my life was worth living, but it did not. I desired to let go of my painful search for my authentic self, but I found phoniness twice as unbearable, so I kept up my pursuit of trying to create a more meaningful life for my family and myself. I wanted to know what it was like to have a healthy appreciation for others, and for myself. Brené Brown calls it "wholehearted living."

Through it all, I was driven by a desire to know myself. I had no idea where to start a search for self-esteem. Bitterness, disorganized patterns of thought, unhealthy behaviors, and hostility hover over my inner world. I had zero understanding of self-worth and integrity. My inner voice kept insisting that change was impossible for me. I believed first- and second-hand victimization had been imposed upon me far too young and far too long. I had seen so much abuse that I learned to believe in my own worthlessness much too early. Consciously and unconsciously, I believed that my toxic and twisted background had damaged my chances of repair. I toyed with the idea that maybe my seeds of virtue had somehow been so tainted that they could not be restored.

Eventually, a brief, faint thought fluttered through my mind, suggesting I now leave the sham of a marriage. My little son was three years old. The thought was profound and convincing enough for me to make a decision to obey the order that very day. It seemed I had played house one minute too long. "Enough my soul seemed to chokingly cry out." I had become bored with the charade of it all. Years earlier, I had missed my chance to play, and yet there I was playing a grown-up's role. The excitement was eluding me, and I didn't know the rules. I felt as if I was in an emotional straitjacket, again. Irate thoughts would come and go without warning. How could I get rid of the intrusive thoughts in my head?

One day, I thought *just suppose I naively trust the wrong mental messages or messengers!* I didn't know how to figure out when I was having useful, intelligent ideas and when I was caught in self-defeating emotional feedback loops. I was terrified that I could end up living a worse life than the one from which I had already escaped.

One minute I was screaming and throwing things. The next minute I was suffocated by my own muffled anger. My screaming festering loneliness seemed to be smothering me. An inescapable sense of stale shame, coupled with boundless resentments, oppressed me. At the same time, my ignorance and relentless anxiety held me captive. I felt as though I were drowning in a deep pool of unlivable anxiety and stress.

Once my cageful outbursts subsided, I'd sit, exhausted, and reflect on the fruitless outbreak. I knew this burst of anger was not an answer, although I wanted it to be. Deep within, I also knew this behavior was not me, even though I did not know what behavior *was* me. As I surveyed the broken household items scattered over the floor, it gave me something to do: clean it up! I would begin to sweep and plot on how to replace the visible evidence of another Madwoman-in-the-Attic-on-a-rampage episode. My inner pain raged unrestrained. I had learned a few things while I was busy working in the family business, but problem solving was not one of them. I needed to strike out at something or someone. Several days later I would find employment for income to replace what had been broken. In one way, it gave me the incentive to seek employment again and again, until I would apply for employment without the breaking cycles of anger, violence, and regret; what self-trickery. I would repeat this concocted behavior time after time during the short three-year marriage. The throwing outbursts were short lived and remained behind me when I terminated the brief and only semi-safe marriage. I would search madly within, trying to figure out why I was behaving in a way that was not me at all. It frustrated me because *I did not know what I did not know.* The mood swings were different, difficult, and exhausting. Controlling my emotions became my new tentative assignment.

The marriage, social drinking, and my numbness decreased my ability to learn how to live beyond my inner messy moments of agony and poor perception of life and living. My truth was waiting to join me; when and where I did not know. One day I realized I did not need to wait, escape, or hide from my inner demons any longer.

My life was going nowhere. I had taken on one minimum wage odd job after another. My fears and discontentment were always my only support system. I was upset with my less than successful accomplishments. After all, I was now twenty-two years old. Naively I had expected much more from me without investigating my belief s, thoughts, or behaviors. I had expected to be happy and filled with many gifts of understanding and purpose.

In the fall of 1969, I had become a single parent. In my mind I had renewed my determination to change my outlook on life. I slowly entered a worse state of mind before I walked away from the upstairs room and the marriage. I spent the next eight years primarily focused on examining my irate behavior. I wanted to obtain better coping skills. I hoped that the physical and mental characteristics I wanted were obtainable. My search was on to make some small self-developmental progress. I had spent eleven years working sixteen-hour days, cut off from normal, healthy human interaction living. I had learned little if anything while in the marriage. I wondered when I was going to get to know "me." I wanted to be released from what I thought I knew, to be free to embrace making daily wiser choices. This required something I knew I did not have, but I was willing to seek out ways to learn and grow so I would know how to adopt change when it was needed. A greater – grander, larger, more generous, happier self was what I desired. Over time, I learned that freedom is not free at all in the beginning of change. It takes determined commitment, focused action, asking for help, dedicated time, self-acceptance, grit, guts, some good-byes to fears, hellos to tears, and some great coaches. I had never heard of the terms open-minded or closed-minded. But, I knew when I heard the term open-minded, I instinctively knew that being a narrow and closed-minded thinker was not a good thing. I had no idea how to rid myself of the constricted and negative thought patterns that seemed to own me; but I was willing to do the necessary research and practice myself into a new way of believing, thinking, and behaving. Learning to let go of the feelings of rejection my parents had imposed upon me was a slow and awkward process. I had finally learned of a few men and women that model a different way of living, and I wanted what they had. I was not real sure just what they had, but I knew I desired it; I wanted a psychic change for myself. Much later in my life my confidence gradually began to glow and slowly grow.

Chapter 7 - **For the Love of Music: 1969**

Listening to the Jim Dancy Radio Show on KPRS during my earlier disheartening my eleven year hauling experience more tolerable. I found great solace in music; it served as an acceptable remedy for my nonexistent spiritual understanding. KPRS was the only African American radio station west of the Mississippi River in 1950. I could not imagine why the soothing sounds of the radio embraced me so energetically. Today I know it had been the only source of urban music and communication I heard daily. The radio shows, games, and music kept me company from 1953 to 1964 primarily. As a young child, when I headed out the back door to climb into one truck or another, many times, after hearing songs like "Ain't That a Shame," "Going to Kansas City," and "Blueberry Hill," all by Fats Domino, I felt ready to make the long nightly challenge from four p.m. to past midnight. Music was the one source of energy which had made me believe I could survive *anything*! Sometimes it was the words, sometimes it was the melodies, and sometimes it was both.

Motown had begun producing music that provided urban energy, primarily to the African American community. Music gave me a soft glimpse of what decent, healthy living might entail. The music offered me the possibility that happiness and hope might someday be within my reach. Most of the songs told collective stories of unmet dreams. One song in particular, "I Don't Hurt Any More," by Dinah Washington, gave me the hope that maybe hurt and pain were temporary. Other songs seemed to share how-to information, such as "Get a Job," and "Take It One Heart Beat at a Time," by Smokey Robinson; "My Girl," by the Temptations; and "Your Precious Love," by Jerry Butler.

Listening to music was my invisible bridge to move beyond my lack of knowledge with bewilderment and curiosity until I could begin the challenging work of learning how to learn. Oprah found true meaning in books while I found true meaning, understanding, and connection from listening to lyrics and harmonious rhythms. Deep within, I knew the experiences the artists were singing about wouldn't happen to me, yet song after song gave me a sense of support while I waited to become the thinking, learning, inquiring person I wanted to be. I could not be satisfied with my lack of knowledge. Both my hunger for information, and my lack of personal growth, tormented me constantly. I often feared I was losing what little ground I had gained in the race to find my always and forever way forward. My unknowingness haunted me mentally. I began to believe that I possibly had some problems larger than life itself. It all was so unnerving.

When I listened to different types of music it made me feel more determined to want to find peace by any means necessary. When the songs ended, however, the strength and desire to change disappeared also. "The Way We Were," by Barbara Streisand, told me that what was too painful to remember, I needed to simply choose to forget. How does one choose to forget when the unforgettable memories are always right there in front of your mind? My pain seemed several miles past unbearable and I wanted to forget, but I couldn't. No one explained the process of forgetting and I didn't know how to figure it out on my own. The songs "You've Got to Change Your Evil Ways," by Carlos Santana, "Evil Woman," by ELO, and "Love Potion Number 9," by the Searchers, each gave me gentle hints of possible solutions for my many seemingly unsolvable issues. Everywhere I turned, I ran into roadblocks of deep bitterness. Most people were indifferent to my emotional injuries, and some even actually hindered me from finding ways to end my unbearable pain. The tangled new and old issues and the unknown change processes kept my progress toward solutions limited. I loved the lyrics and the melodies of "You Got to Change Your Evil Ways," and "Evil Woman." I took both songs personally.

I am still not sure when my chronic boredom turned into an evil craving which I saw operating naturally within my family's interactions. My natural inclination to fight for survival took my uncontrollable anxiousness to an all-time high. I found my evil behavior somehow tied with my desire to survive. I had been allowing my misery to dictate my life. Non-productive activities and cocktails only pushed me further into a baffling level of despair and unhappiness. Nothing made me feel better, and that was the scary part.

Fourteen years later I begin to realize I needed to change my thought life if I wanted to have healthier progress with my outer behavior. I begin to desire to make better choices. As I saw my unacceptable ways dissipates and my surely-goodness-and-mercy life forces slowly become better options this added hope to my struggle. Although my thick fears were holding me tight I was determined to make friends with the change process.

There was something about listening to music that rallied around me to soften my restless spirit, making life more tolerable. Music was my only kinship with the word "love." Music allowed me brief moments to accept necessary good-byes and desperate hellos, to my new adventures, experiences, and practices. I comprehended music through threads of mysterious, mythical, and mystical wonder; I did not understand the great necessity of love and loving as the antidote for hate and hatred. After hearing the last reverberating low soft note of each song, my frantic, psychotic, and chaotic world of reality would reappear instantly, as if the mental chaos had not been suspended just seconds before. I made a commitment to find answers from somebody or something about the work required to settle my mind and my heart so I could build a respectable life worth living. The fast pace of my grueling childhood and the birth of Motown wove a slender thread of tolerance within me. It was a delicate balance, but the mixture offered a small glimmer of hope, again. Hope that I might someday lead a more peaceful existence. This spark was my only defense against the deep misery that engulfed me. I found myself clinging to it like a life raft.

As I listened to the many artists in the music industry during the 60s and 70s, it seemed they themselves began to sing about their bottomless inner pain. Their songs of pain and unrequited love drove me more insane and the lyrics haunted my mind day and night. What little progress I had made was evaporating, and I was losing the will to try for a better life. For these tormented artists, it did not seem that neither money nor fame stopped their deep pain, even as they were vocalizing the words. Everyone seemed to be more concerned with hiding their discomfort than wanting to take steps to eliminate it. No one was advocating that there was another way.

What I know now is that happiness and unhappiness does not discriminate, just as being wealthy and being poor does not discriminate. We each choose the state we wish to live within on some level. At that time, though, I simply did not know how to process my feelings as they slowly awakened one by one from their dormant state. I kept trying to work it out by bouncing from one job to another, relocating, again, and again, and feeling sorry for my seemingly un-blessed self.

I was working as a soda fountain worker at one of the popular Parkview Drug Stores when one day there was a news flash: Presidential candidate Robert Kennedy had been assassinated in the pantry of the Ambassador Hotel. This was in June of 1968. I could not believe so many casualties were happening in the 60s: the four little girls in the Sixteenth Street Baptist Church in September 1963; President John F. Kennedy in November 1963; my first still born child August 11, 1966; and Martin Luther King Jr. in April 1968. I did not know how the joy of living could emerge from such tragedies.

The trail of deaths tormented me. Compounding the torment was the Vietnam War; and I could see people suffering with depression all over the place, just as I suffered silently. The only aspect of hope I could pull from my daily life was Marvin Gaye singing "What's Going On." It seemed that I had experienced greater ruins of physical, spiritual, and mental wreckage than I could reasonably expect to recover from. My second son was now three. I had to make a change in my life again. I had to discover how to become a healthy functional human being. It seemed impossible to find anything worth loving about myself, but I felt it was my duty to learn how to love my child or children. I would ask myself over and over, "How am I to know love's language, its signs, its magnificence, or its legitimacy?" I had asked myself love questions over and over, again and again: What does love feel like? How does one obtain it? If one finds genuine love, how does one keep it from slipping away? I wanted to know; I needed to know. I would wildly search back within my mind hunting for someone – anyone – who had demonstrated love in my neighborhood, community, or environment. I dared not ask such questions aloud.

At the same time, I was trying to understand how to fight loneliness and a spirit of indifference. It was to be many years before I began to see some change in the struggle from hating myself, to a low level of tolerating myself, to eventually a glimpse of liking myself, and finally learning to love myself. Even when I finally realized the energy to love me had happened; it was still – to me - an unbelievable accomplishment, over forty years later.

My most important struggle other than learning to love myself was maintaining employment. The constant workplace tussles defied and vexed me from sixteen to thirty years old. I learned that all that was missing in my life had to be learned from trial and error, not blaming and finding fault within the process. My vivid imagination and almost aggressively unpredictable emotions fought against the thought of confronting my many personal weaknesses and failures. I had heard or read somewhere that each day is a "present," but without knowing my purpose, I had trouble finding anything to appreciate about my new daily twenty-four hour time allotments.

Eventually, I could not help but wonder if trying to adjust to living my life without joy was my real, core problem. Or maybe my core problem was simply having so many unmet needs. Perhaps my once "social" drinking habit (which had long since turned into "necessity drinking") was the primary problem. Or was the primary problem what is now called Oppositional Defiance Disorder (ODD)? I couldn't tell for the life of me what the truth was, but *I needed to know.*

I would drink and think, and think and drink, more and more. Days, weeks, months, and years passed by without any progress at all. I kept trying to separate this new drink and think riddle: "Is my thinking causing my bizarre drinking, or is my drinking causing my bizarre thinking?" It was maddening, to say the least. I was lost in the sense of trying to find a starting place to begin to bring order into my life. I could not figure it out. Therefore, I kept right on drinking and thinking, ad infinitum. The song by the Impressions gave me the vitality to "Keep on Pushing," even when my mind, body and soul was intoxicated with abnormal and normal fears and drinking all day and even in my dreams at night.

I was trying to not give up on learning how to live. I wanted to learn to love. I wanted to learn how to live differently. My narrow definition of "living" was to be content with a life of having a family, cooking, sewing, shopping, and working; this was all I saw demonstrated in my community. Somewhere far in my foggy mind I wanted each new day to be embraced with friendly hellos and end with a spirit of "Thank you, Universe." I wanted a career, not just a job. I wanted to love my children, not just exist in their lives as parent. I wanted to be confident and not so shy it hurt in my stomach. Above all, I wanted to develop a greater degree of emotional, social, and spiritual connection with those around me and within myself.

I wanted to forgive and be forgiven. I wanted empathy and compassion for others and again for myself. I wanted to be loveable and not angry and hateful. I wanted to be the kind of person I would enjoy meeting someday. I wanted to let go of things I could not change. I wanted to be willing to change the things I could. I wanted to be comfortable in my own skin; my own homes' quote unquote, and my own processes, and progress. I wanted to love. I wanted so much more for my life, but the "much" was still unidentifiable, at that time.

I was not sure if love was a natural sensation or if it was a learned emotion. I still wasn't even sure how to define or recognize *love.* Eventually, I learned that most behaviors are learned by continual repetition. I do not remember when I discovered the need to practice, to pretend, to "act as if." I learned that "acting as if" was a key factor for change. Acting my way into a different way of thinking soon led to true self-discipline, and finally, healthier emotions were no longer foreign to me. It then became easier to respond to others in a healthier way than what I had experienced as a child.

In later years, I was able to separate my wants from my needs somewhat. Temporarily, I had to refer to my parents as my gatekeepers after the forgiveness process was underway. I noticed that whenever I referred to my parents as "parents," a vengeful feeling would stir up within me again and again in every corner of my mind in response to being reminded about their unmerciful management of my life and their family expectations. Assigning them the title "gatekeepers" was the only way I could give my mind a mental break from them in order to heal from the impact of their emotional and physical wrath.

I desperately needed to give them a break in order to give myself permission to keep moving forward. Their actions and personalities were theirs, not mine; it was not helpful to hide behind them in order to avoid facing my personal challenges.

I felt a similar response whenever I reminisced about traits my mother once displayed. The many negative traits which had replaced my mother's formerly optimistic qualities were difficult to accept. She had been steadfast, adaptable, ambitious, flexible, and giving. Her striving for the good life was lost in my father's obsession with the hauling business. Even though she quit working in that business with him, it left her mentally and physically worn, torn and beat up; she became a wretched person. Her sense of optimism and joy never returned before her death. She lost the will to care as the demands on her for love and attention grew. I believe she settled or made the mistake of making her husband her God. The responsibility thrust upon her to serve as wife, mother, and provider was too great to carry alone. My father's early attributes included being hardworking, faithful, and dedicated to a fault. But he lost the motivation to be a helpmate to his wife and loving parent to his children.

I was very much aware of my debilitating struggle to accept conditions as they were. I was equally aware of my inability to ignore the depth of the ongoing discomforts. Blind obedience generally leaves little room for healthy self-governing solutions. There were too many painful daily calamities to not feel the pressure.

My parents devised, designed, and implemented ways to support their family economically, but they seemed to have no plan or ability for supporting us in any other fashion. I was determined to live a better lifestyle when I grew up; this was my only pledge of allegiance – to me. I knew I would raise my children differently, but I knew I would make my mistakes too. My imperfections would be my guide toward self-betterment.

About four years later, when my son was about seven years old, he somehow ended up at his grandfather's last remaining recycling yard. I happened to be driving by the area, lost in my own thoughts. I looked out the window casually while waiting for the red light to change at an intersection. I noticed a little dirty-faced boy with a small sack leaving the corner store. I thought to myself, that little boy's face looks unkempt just like mine had looked when I was a child. I stared more intently and realized that it was my son. I pulled the car over to the side and picked up my child. I stopped by the place he was returning to. It was the once enormous booming family business, now at a different location. We said good bye and went on our merry way.

I am sure with all of the mayhem in my life, my son hanging out with his grandfather had happened indirectly; perhaps I had left him with another family member and they had an emergency of some sort that could not wait, and they found it necessary to take him to my parents' residence. I do know my father had taken him as a helper because his health was failing, just as my mother's health had failed her earlier. When my parents purchased their last new home, it was not located in a business-zoned district. What was left of the hauling business, one small recycling yard, was located on the other end of town.

Years later, I began to study, search, and research to gain more knowledge concerning attributes, skills, abilities, emotions, moods, and character building. I needed to rid myself of the hostility I had developed trying to survive my harsh, unkind, and distasteful childhood. Amen. At last, what needed to happen finally happened: it was done! Mostly I prayed, "Thank you, God, for you led the way back via Calvary."

Photographs

Very few early photographs of me survive.
I am grateful to have these to share with you.

Leona: age 2-3

Leona - approx. age 4

Richard (age 5) and Secret (age 2)

Leona and the kids: Albuquerque, 1976-77

Leona - after the miracle (approx. age 41)

Leona - college graduation (2003)

My mother, Mattie, at age 67

Chapter 8 - **Hollywood Styles: 1971**

I enrolled in a cosmetology course in 1964, completed the course, and received my license. I worked odd jobs here and there until 1969. Then, at the young age of twenty-three, I became a business owner, opening the Hollywood Styles Beauty and Barber Salon. It took four months to refurbish the back room of what had previously been a barbershop. The process of finishing the new addition to the shop would be complete after removing the adhesive residue from the newly tiled floor. Tragically, the worker had forgotten to turn off the automatic overhead heater while using a cleaning product clearly marked "Do Not Use Near Open Flame." As the worker was finishing his job, the heating unit automatically switched on. In less than a split second, the shop exploded into a ferocious firestorm. The entire place turned into a glowing and growing inferno. I was so petrified I could not will myself to leave the building. The exit door which was open slammed shut with a powerful swoosh from the change in air pressure. Once the door slammed shut, I walked slowly to the door and just stood inside with my back against the door looking at the worker on the floor. The worker screamed, "Open that door!" several times as he lay on the floor of the burning building; his pants were literally on fire. The container which had the flammable liquid inside had toppled over from the blast and soaked one of his pant legs. As the flames raced up the walls and spread across the ceiling, the worker's clothing had caught fire. The worker soon scrambled to the closed door and yanked it open; his pants were still in flames. I followed him out of the burning building. I can't say when he stopped, dropped, and rolled as we had been taught in fire drills and safety manuals. If he had done it before we got out of the building, we both would likely have died.

By now the firefighters had arrived. They aimed their powerful, thick, larger-than-life water hoses into the building. A vast stream of water was quickly sprayed through the salon's opened door and drenched the fire until it was out, leaving the once beautiful salon completely destroyed by fire, smoke, and water. As I stood outside the smoldering building, I remember thinking *I've got to find another way!*

Oddly, this harrowing incident was not a setback for me. I still felt so undeserving that I was not sure I wanted to be a part of such a promising opportunity. Truthfully, I was glad to be back at the beginning of the rebuilding process. I was comfortable with beginnings. However, as I stood outside the ruins of the burned building, safe and without harm, this was the moment I recall having my first intense craving for a drink ever. I was twenty-three.

I had always been obsessed with continually wanting and needing something. I just was not sure what it was I wanted or needed so much of the time. This time, though, I had a vague, unfamiliar urge of wanting and needing a drink. I hadn't been afraid of real harm or danger; only imaginary harm or danger made me afraid. My early conditioning had been more animalistic than human. In less than six months, Hollywood Styles was rebuilt. Rebuilding the shop was extremely energizing for me, but by the time the shop was open for business, I had lost my small desire to be a part of the business. I did not have a "plan B." Lack of a back-up plan seemed unfortunate to me then, but I stayed with plan A longer than I might have otherwise, and that meant I was learning and developing skills even if I didn't fully appreciate it at the time.

I quickly built a great clientele once the salon was up and running. I had standing appointments each day like clockwork. There was a jukebox with all the number-one Motown hits. Clients loved dropping their coins in the slot, choosing their favorite tunes, and entertained us all with their dancing before they swayed and sashayed back to their seat. It was a fun social hour experience. The shop was a business ahead of its time.

Sometimes the shop's co-owner would raise the cover of the jukebox and set it on auto play, especially in the late afternoon on weekends. The police would routinely stop and ask us to tone it down. The neighborhood could hear James Brown screaming "Please, Please, Please" on the juke box. For most people, this would have been a fun place to work or spend time; however, I noticed a depressed feeling lingering over me as the days, weeks, and months passed.

This entire salon episode lasted maybe a year and a half. One day I could no longer stand myself, the salon, the music, the staff, or the clients. I did not want to live, but if the cosmos was going to force me to stick around, this depressing state of mind had to go. An uncomfortable emotional ache in the pit of my stomach would not go away; it just relentlessly drained me of my spirit. Even drinking beer brought little or no relief.

I wanted to be happy. Most people in my circle seemed to be comfortable pretending to be happy, but not truly being happy. I wondered why people were pretending to have fun, pretending to know God, pretending to be okay with who they were so much of the time. People within my environment seemed content with retail business and public interaction as a way of life. That seemed so superficial and unfulfilling to me. I didn't know it then, but I was an introvert operating under an outgoing and cheery façade.

Preoccupation with my past and present miseries demanded my attention even more than primping one hairstyle after another. Trying to shield my uncomfortable state of mind from my customers was a difficult job all by itself. Even serving an affluent clientele was not satisfying enough for me to ignore my quest for something more meaningful, something better and different, although I still did not know what I was looking for. The curriculum of the academy of cosmetology I attended had not offered lessons in customer service practices on any level. Still, I did the best I could to cover my angst and keep my patrons satisfied.

My customers were filled with exuberance. They had seemed enchanted with their new stylist and the salon's trendy, warm, energetic atmosphere. They tipped large tips. I kept thinking I should have been happy, but my internal doubts kept dampening the joy I might have otherwise felt from the happiness and excitement of my customers. It was all too crazy and conflicting. The collision of my shattered nerves and perplexing thoughts with the excessive chatter of my clients eventually became too much. I was too restless to let my life stop there. I started to contemplate an escape.

By early 1972, I had decided the beauty world was not for me. The profession itself bored me to distraction. I kept thinking I should have been able to tolerate the innate repetitiveness of hairdressing longer than I did; I had – after all – sorted trash for a solid decade, but that was not the biggest problem. My real problem was I did not know how to be a social butterfly. I had no basic social skills to summon and my inner turmoil kept me from cultivating useful relationships with my co-workers and customers. Many-a-day I had walked out during my beauty salon shifts. Finally, one day, indifferent to anyone's response, I just said "Hasta luego!" and walked out for the last time. I never returned.

Under different circumstances, the salon could very well have been a place of contentment for me, but it was not. I could see the handwriting on the wall, so to speak, of my potential endangerment if I continued to work in a setting where I felt so out of place. I couldn't keep faking it; I needed to find work in a place where I could be alone, where it was quiet where I could feel like a worker among many other workers. The salon was just too busy and intense and intimate for me.

The 1972 chartbuster movie "Across 110th Street" had nothing on Hollywood Styles Beauty and Barber Salon once it was reopened. The energetic and trendy atmosphere offered excitement and controlled chaos, and the remarkable services drew in a popular, upper echelon clientele. The combination of those elements spelled success on many levels, especially lucrative sales. Hollywood Styles was one hell of a beauty and barber salon and stood out among salons in the Midwest for a short while.

The salon was a high energy spot for early hipsters before and after I moved on, but I had grown uncomfortable, and my discomfort was intensifying to the point that I felt I was in danger somehow. I was not hip by any definition; "square," that was me. I felt so out of place that I needed to get away from the salon environment. I often wondered, "Who was in more danger, them or me?" I never got an answer to that question.

After I left the salon business, I became an employee at one of the well-known hospitals in the neighborhood for several weeks. I thought that might be a predictable, steady, quiet atmosphere where I could just do my assigned work and not be bothered by any of the other employees, but I was wrong.

It was later heartbreaking to remember the supervisor's disbelief over my nonchalant attitude when she called because I had not shown up for work. I calmly informed her that I was not coming in that day, or any other day. I did not wait for her to respond. I was exhausted from trying to be an adult. I could not tell her that I walked on and off jobs like people change their socks. I struggled to simply say "Good morning" in response to my co-workers when they greeted me. I often wondered if some people believed I was trying to be aloof, but that wasn't it. I was simply socially paralyzed and riddled with a high level of anxiety.

After I left the salon business, I began to have nightmares. I had occasionally experienced nightmares since living upstairs; now they were occurring more and more frequently. I had the same two nightmares over and over; they would not go away. One was a never ending, disturbing streetcar ride. The other found me floating inside a seemingly bottomless dark pit. Apparently, I was trying to lose my parents' grip on me even in my dreadful dreams. It seemed that the bottomless dark pit was my attempt to escape the gatekeepers also; I was looking for a place of comfort and joy, even as I was dead to the world. I could not tell if I was trying to accept defeat, trying to surrender, or trying to ignore the awful fact that I knew I was failing miserably at getting my life assignments right.

I was looking through streetcar windows while running from my parents in my dreams. Was I trying to hide in the ginormous, bottomless, pitch-black, dark tunnel, trying to lose them or lose me? Or was I simply seeking salvation from my manufactured fears? The scary streetcar and black pit nightmares were both regular and highly disturbing. Somehow, I received some kind of indirect prompting of sorts indicating that I was going to have the nightmares prior to going to sleep.

No one on or off the streetcars tried to help me with any of my public drama. On the other hand, in the bottomless pit nightmare only I was available to help me. I was so preoccupied and distracted by the gyration of descending downward in the wide, deep pit, inch by inch, that the focus on saving me was my only immediate concern. Both nightmares left me stunned for several hours after I awoke. Ironically, the nightmares each held a different meaning for me, but the same earth-shattering terror. The nightmares switched back and forth. I never knew which would begin to play when I shut my eyes.

In the streetcar nightmare, the streetcars always traveled back and forth on Brooklyn Avenue. It was the place where I had lived until I was nineteen. It was the same street where I had sat upstairs near the window watching cars passing by for entertainment. It was the same place from which I had finally walked down the winding stairs and out the door for the last time, without a choice or a plan. In the frightening nightmare, I was always being chased, harassed, and assailed by my parents.

I would be seated in about the fourth row, in the outside seat on the right-hand side, about two rows from the back door of the moving, packed streetcar. I'd look up and there they were, my parents, the two of them lurching toward me. Sometimes they carried vague-looking weapons, raised high in the air. Looks of scorn covered their faces.

They walked with haste. I called it speed walking. "Speedy" had been my nickname; Speedy. They would glare directly at me. I'd look at them with quick double-take glances as they approached me from either the back or front of the streetcar as I dashed from my seat, time and time again. They seemed close enough to grab me most of the time. I would spring from my seat in one twist and run toward the closest exit, depending on the direction from which they were coming toward me. I would jump to freedom from the streetcars, one step to the sidewalk, and keep running.

In the nightmares, I would run like a maniac to the next streetcar just ahead of the streetcar I had vacated and then leap inside. Trying to lose the two angry parents was my daily focus. Most times, no sooner than I had reached my fourth-row seat, I'd look up and there they would be again, rushing toward me, and it started all over.

Sometimes I would look to the back of the streetcar, and there they would be, coming toward me from the back. Again, I would spring from my seat and run out the front door. When I jumped from the moving streetcars, I never thought whether I should run to catch another car in front of the one I had just left. The decision was somehow made for me in my panic. I would just allow my fight-or-flight instincts to carry and protect me. I was terribly afraid of both options and feared for my life. The gatekeepers took turns leading the pursuit. They always showed up together, every time; a serious tag-team witch hunt. The nightmares always started at the same scene where they had ended previously; as if someone had pressed *pause* and then *play*.

I wondered if my real living experiences were my commercial breaks. I always knew when a night of bad dreams was coming because just before going to bed I would notice the peculiar and familiar feeling of being inside the nightmare. When that feeling came to me, I would wander around trying to prolong staying awake. That feeling before sleep, warning me that the streetcar nightmare was going to replay, beckoned me to come into its frightening grip! I had these feelings so many times; it seemed like millions.

One night in 1977, I did not want to re-experience or be traumatized by the streetcar nightmare, not one more time. I was tired. I did not want to be held captive in the powerful throes of yet another trauma dream all over again. My physical hours awake seemed nothing more than live nightmares themselves. I did not want the same mayhem feeling when I fell asleep! I did not want to feel the heartbreaking, breathtaking, and soul-shaking powerless moments again. I did not want to feel myself physically wrestling to awaken from the nightmare's intensity while I was still deeply asleep.

Trying to ignore the ominous, repetitive, warnings time and time again was wearing me down. I'd tried to be brave and allowed myself to drift into the nightmares many times before. Moments later I would be twisting, turning, struggling, trying to awaken myself to end the vicious encounters. I had attempted on numerous occasions to wake up, and it was always a hopeless struggle. I was outweighed by some force greater than myself. I was always without the power to turn the channel or wake up. I was forced to wait until the dream ended, and then I would have to sit up to catch my breath, to try to shake off the entire occurrence. The nightmare was intimidating each time. For ten years or so I had tried to make peace with the streetcar dream.

The nightmare dreams had begun in 1966 as I sat waiting upstairs on Brooklyn Street, trying to stay awake until daybreak, after the death of my first child. It was one of the reasons I began to stay awake all night and sleep during the day. I somehow believed as time passed that I would be able to handle the nightmare more courageously during the day, if I must have it.

Not having anyone to tell about my mental struggles made the nightmare experiences far more unnerving. I hated having the nightmare when I was out of town; it made trying to re-establish my bearings more difficult. It would always take several hours for me to calm myself once I had awakened from a nightmare session.

When the unsettling streetcar nightmare took breaks, another new recurring dreadful nightmare replaced it. There was a large, seemingly bottomless, dark pit. I would awake within the dream, circling around in a downward spiraling motion. The tunnel was wide beyond description, larger than I could comprehend. I could not see the inner roundness of its walls, yet I knew I was circling within an enclosed, open-topped unit; only God knew why. The inner diameter of the circle seemed double that of a Ferris wheel, or maybe larger. I would float with my arms outstretched, like a flying bird. I could tell somehow that I was close to the invisible walls while in motion; but I could not touch the wall-like interior. The gigantic funnel was a blend of dark sky and cloud-like substance. I am not sure how I discerned the makeup of the funnel, for it was pitch black inside.

The second nightmare was intense but did not plague me as regularly as the streetcar dream. I floated around slowly within the tunnel. I floated downward in centimeter increments; with each complete circle I would drop lower. It took a long time to make a complete circle. I could feel the vibration as my body spiraled mercilessly downward around the inner edge toward the bottom of the pit. Instinctively, I decided the pit was bottomless. While in motion I could only imagine its depth. I did not want to acquaint myself with the actual dimensions of the pit. Somehow, I knew it was dangerously deep. I could see it was incredibly wide. The farther down toward the invisible bottom I moved, the more apprehensive I became. Sometimes I contemplated staying closer to the upper edge of the funnel just in case I wanted to attempt to pull myself out before I descended too low. As I was preparing for bed one night in the early fall of 1977, a solution came to mind. I had the usual intuition that informed me that I would have the dream. I'd had the signal many times before, and I had grown familiar with the warnings. I was moving toward the bed, and I stood still near the bed I was preparing to climb into. I was ready to kneel and say my new nightly prayer, *Thank you*, and then get into bed. As I stood there between kneeling and anticipating another episode of the streetcar drama, my instinct suggested I let the gatekeepers catch me. The thought repeated itself twice. The messenger ended the message with, *After all, you have not done anything to them.* I pondered this advice. *Yes! I haven't done anything to them.* I climbed into bed with much confidence and waited and waited for a short while for the dream to come. I wanted to see for myself what my parents wanted. I almost welcomed them to come running into my dream space. I drifted off to sleep that night and both nightmares drifted away. Forty-one years later, they haven't returned.

I still remember the last time I had the streetcar nightmare. I was trying to not drink alcohol and had succeeded for several months. As part of my coping strategy, I had been told to pray "Please" in the morning, and "Thank You" at night. It was working.

I can't say just when I began having the second nightmare, but I do know when both nightmares terminated themselves. The two nightmares had played over and over at random for years and now they were gone.

I experienced a relief like never before! There were no goodbyes; the nightmares just disappeared, like magic. At two different seasons in my life the two nightmares had appeared. I guess announcing "The End" is not allowed at the end of nightmares; perhaps that happens only in movies.

I had left a number of jobs because I was feeling trapped, and I left my marriage for similar reasons. After leaving the marriage, many unspeakable experiences suggested I should return. I knew better. Being on my own was terrifying but hiding from my old frustrations was no longer an option. That part of my life was over. I now had a brand new set of morning and night frustrations. Being single was difficult, but in truth I had always been on my own.

One day, when my despair was more than I could bear, I received a message from within which gently instructed me to locate one of my Sunday school teachers and request prayer. I obeyed the message.

Once I located my teacher, I told her what was happening based on my years of fears and stormy mental deficiencies. I tried to tell her before she began to pray that the prayer thing was not going to work. The results were astonishing. This incident with prayer did not renew my faith; it was just a spiritual emergency call. I was shocked; I did not even slightly believe in prayer at that time, not at all. In five minutes or less I received some last-minute instructions from her. I thanked her and thrust myself back into my turbulent world of bare minimum survival.

The prayer time had worked. She gave me one scripture to read and think about: Psalms 116 1:19.[4] I read it to death. It seemed that I was searching for a place where I could live with less shame and guilt. As an adult I had grown tired of having traumatic, intense, and destructive fears as my only close companions. The more satanic ones formed groups and followed me as I entered slumber land for midnight rendezvouses. Some characters were hanging out all night long, first here and then there. Some of the most ferocious-looking characters stood in doorways with their hands on their hips, lips poked out, and necks jerking as they conversed with no one in particular. There were other loud-mouthed participants looking in and out of the windows waiting for decisions to be made by someone else. My, they were an active bunch.

For me, in real life, the time of hanging out at house parties, on porches, and trying to get the hang of sitting on bar stools in night clubs was over. My living room once or twice became my well-lit drinking spot briefly in the midnight hours. I also noticed that when I drank, I was provoked by my inner gang to get in my car and drive somewhere, anywhere. I caught the insane drift and put a halt to the driving insanity. The last drive left an impression on me: I side swiped about four parked cars, returning to my living room after the midnight drive.

In my constantly frantic mind, depending on the degree of my crisis at hand, real or fictitious, spiritual disorders, unaccountability, or any other fleeting occurrences, second by

---

[4] The full text of this Psalm appears at the end of this book.

second it was a critical mass production. And, if the gang in my head could not get me all riled up instantly, we would all travel into my past to wake up some unfinished, psychologically unresolved dispute to wallow in.

It was as if I was afraid to be calm and okay. I could not figure out the difference between silence and boredom. The need to be disturbed had become my master. At this time in my life I ceased to go to the movies. The self-induced movies within my head were beyond entertaining. Some movies were without endings; they would just fade in and out at will. I moved from Kansas City, Missouri. The Jazz City had flourished even in the depths of the Great Depression. Someone once said, "If you want to see some sin, go to Kansas City, not Paris." I concluded they were speaking of Kansas City, Missouri, not Kansas City, Kansas. However, I moved to Kansas City, Kansas just across the Missouri River after seeing more sin in me than any spiritual or unspiritual laws allowed.

Chapter 9 - I Needed to Know: 1972

Still searching frantically for a place of comfort, I began to relocate more frequently, as if I was driven by some vicious, uncontrollable mania. It was unnerving for me to live anyplace past thirty, sixty or ninety days. I had no idea how to remain planted through times of order or disorder. I remember thinking, "Since I can't stop relocating from place to place in town, I might as well leave town." I relocated from Kansas City Missouri, to Kansas City, Kansas, in 1972.

I felt like I was being held captive in a zone of intense panic. I knew my case was different in ways that made things much more difficult for me. I was tired of multiple hardships dictating my life. I was preoccupied with finding an easy solution to solve my complicated thoughts rather always being forced to deal with my unmanageable physical life. It was difficult to engage in planning a healthy future for myself. I was preoccupied about my tomorrows only because each present day was so uncomfortable and filled with disorder. Deep within, though, I leaned toward the impossible and hoped it would become possible for me someday.

I decided to return to the place where I once had brief feelings of contentment. Yes, I would return to church, like a prodigal daughter, one more time, I thought. It was late September of 1972. I was now immeasurably frustrated and anxious. The church idea was my hope for salvation for the moment. *Let's go back to church,* I thought again. When I had attended church before, I had found a dark, shadowy kind of hope, but it was hope nonetheless. I was searching for a way out of my deplorable mental disarray. Maybe this time it would help.

Maybe everyone was pretending there was a God, I thought, with my best possible mindset at that time. I'd vaguely reasoned to myself more than a few times that maybe I needed to join in and accept my pretend belief as genuine, and call playacting my version of truth, belief, or faith. I was tired of wasting my valuable time seemingly getting nowhere despite my urgency for change. The church folks in the congregations I frequented made knowing God themselves a priority but seemed somewhat challenged when trying to promote their message of conviction to others. Who was I to want more personal experience, confirmation, and insight about God? I learned to pretend and keep it moving. I also made a silent commitment to cease all drinking of alcoholic beverages to myself while attending church, this time. After several weeks of attending church had passed, I became more and more agitated. I moved with a sense of being prodded by some new determined energy. I wanted to change my agnostic stance on religious matters. My judgement of religious references bothered and distracted me far too deeply; I wanted the continual religious and spiritual debates within me to cease.

I told myself to look forward to the church experience one more time. Perhaps I had missed something in my many church travels. I wanted to leave the chaotic life I had and try to make going to church and religious practices my reality. I wanted a life worth living, and I had no idea what that looked or felt like. I had no idea where to start in changing the disjointed, disoriented living lifestyle I had grown accustomed to. I did not know where or how to begin my self-development process, and the new church experience was a total distraction from my search for a better me. No matter what I tried, I felt that they weren't willing to meet me where I was, a wretch undone.

In truth, I had never left the church setting totally. Wherever I was living, church was always calling my name. I visited many churches during my many phases of mental and physical breakdowns and recovery. In all that time, I was not able to find not one iota of hope, faith, or love in my quest for comfort from the church.

I did not feel welcomed at the church, but I never felt welcomed anywhere. I kept telling myself it was nothing personal; I felt unwelcome regardless of where I was. Still, even with all the feelings of not fitting in, I kept trying to make church life work, attending whatever church seemed open for servicing souls, trying to live by the teachings I was hearing. Nothing worked. Eventually, I reached the conclusion that my soul was not included in the church's loss prevention strategy; I was not on the list to be saved.

I now believe church services are among the many places for serving lost souls, but they aren't the only places where one can find healing and acceptance. It's like attending prayer meeting services. Some churches even offer self-leadership classes. I often wondered if being filled with the Holy Spirit was just another consumer product or special service the church offered.

Somehow, I was not equipped with the necessary weapons to fight off my noisy religious confusion. Neither could I surrender my deep doubts about subscribing to popular religion as a solution to my troubles. My inner debate teams were not backing down either way. So, I just kept rolling along, picking up thoughts and feelings of unrest and becoming recklessly crazier by the millisecond.

Joining the church with all of my brokenness and self-pity did not solve my grave mental problems; as a matter of fact, it intensified my emotional mess. Once settled in the church routine, I began to rededicate my life over and over and over every time the altar call was made. I attended every service I could attend, seven days a week. I wanted a "quicker than quick" fix, so I could get on with my life. It seemed like there was not enough forgiveness for the kind of redemption and reconciliation I needed, wanted, and seriously believed I was entitled to. I wanted a deliverance of heart and mind. I wanted a testimony of change.

I began to participate in many of the church activities and devotional services. I wanted spiritual makeover, and I wanted it fast. I was trying to straighten up, make up, and clean up my life the only way I knew, which was to saturate myself in church activities. I tried my best to ignore my mental state. Was I fit to be a child of the Almighty with all of my imperfections? I tried to want to be me, even with my shattered heart, my undernourished body, and my disturbed spirit.

After three or four months, I could tell my commitment to forcing real change was losing momentum. I knew I was slowly spinning out of control one more time. My intentional restoration process was still in its early stages, but the out-of-control signs were there. I began to crave a drink in order to fortify myself, so I could mix with some of the self-righteous church folks and not let my anger seep out in ways that weren't church-like, forget Christ-like.

I had grown used to being out of control and it felt much more "normal" than being in-control; control spelled and seemed like boredom. I was in search of many personal attributes that seemed to be missing from my life, but one in particular was self-control. I was losing my resolve, though. I first realized that I "needed" to drink in 1973. prior to that I believed I drank because I chose too. My thirty-day commitment was weak and stressful. I could tell I was not making any progress with not drinking or with the church. My body was there but my mind refused to follow.

I stayed with the church for a few more months.

The pastor asked for volunteers to make phone calls. I needed a drink to volunteer. I needed a drink to cope with all of the qualities I did not have. I decided to try to fulfill the task. The next day was Monday, a holiday, and I was off work. I was working as a clerk typist in an office on the fourteenth floor of a luxurious high-rise office building in downtown Kansas City, Missouri. I lived in Kansas City, Kansas, but still took the bus back across the Missouri River five days a week to work, and I was still scared to death of everything and everybody, everywhere I went.

Although I lived within walking distance of Pleasant Green Baptist Church, I apprehensively drove the three or four blocks to the meeting house. My professional, social, and public fears were fighting against me, but I persevered. My little son and I walked up the church steps and into the foyer. I was welcomed by one of the church sisters. "Good morning, how can I help you?" she said.

I stated my reason for being there on a Monday morning: I had come to fulfill my volunteer promise to make phone calls.

We walked down the stairs into the extra-large, well-lit conference room. The church also had a bowling alley in the same area. My son had found his way behind the wall where the bowling pins repositioned themselves several Sundays earlier. I had freaked out. I did not want him to get hurt on my watch, but he seemed determined. We entered one of the smaller side rooms. There was a nice large desk and chair and an old-fashioned dial phone; on the desk lay a sheet of instructions for what to say, and a contact list. I left my son in the large room to wander around. I thought surely he'd be safe outside the small office where I could hear and see him while I made the phone calls.

I sat in the desk chair. I pulled the top drawer open, looking for a pencil or pen; nothing there. Just when I was about to give up, the church sister poked her head back into the room and said, "You may need these." She gave me several yellow number two pencils and red ink pens. I was instructed to draw a line through wrong or disconnected numbers and place a red check mark by the actual contacts made. I was to leave the list for the next volunteer to work with later.

I was moving down the columns quite rapidly; at ten in the morning, most people were either not answering their phone or they were allowing their answering machines to take the call.

A lot of the numbers were bad for one reason or another. I quickly learned all the varieties of pre-recorded telephone company messages: "This number is no longer in service," "Please check the number you are calling and dial it again," or "The number you are trying to reach has been disconnected or changed." I also heard "The new number is not listed" quite frequently. The few times I spoke with a real person, the responses were usually rude, cold, or quite cruel. Still, I explained my reason for calling, thanked them for their information, and disconnected so I could dial the next number. Each time I called a number on that list, I almost felt as if I was trying to dial God's number for help.

I was getting ready to dial another call when I heard a loud thump come from the recreation hall outside of the small office. Instinctively, I knew the old heavy piano base I had seen leaning against the wall in the other room was involved. When my son and I had first entered the building, I had given it a quick glance as we walked past and tried to ignore the potential danger of the piano. I wanted to believe my imagination was signaling a false alarm. I knew I was being over-sensitive because I was so uncomfortable, so I had focused my attention on my shaky-nerves, the secretary who was giving me instructions, and my work on the phone call project.

I spun around and leaped from my chair. I ran the few steps through the doorway of the small office into the large conference room. As I had feared, there lay Richard, pinned underneath the heavy piano frame. His head was free of the piano's base structure, but his body was pinned from the chest down. I gasped, then began yelling for someone to come and help! I tried to raise the piano myself, but there were two huge supporting braces on each side of him. I could not raise and pull at the same time. Soon others arrived to help.

Someone called 9-1-1. The paramedics arrived quickly, but by the time they got there, Richard had been freed from beneath the piano. Because of the two ten-inch supportive braces holding the frame up off the floor, his little chest was undamaged; it appeared to be completely untouched. I noticed a shift from panic to relief, and then to the realization that this was the first time others had ever rushed to assist me. With this feeling of help, I detected – perhaps for the first time – the depth of my lifelong trauma: that brief moment of support, though it came from utter strangers, was like a breath of fresh air. Was this going to be yet another addition to my already traumatized state? Although I was grateful the incident was not fatal, I was not able to feel what would have normally been the jolt of comprehension of the seriousness of the incident.

Why had it required a near tragedy for me to feel compassion from others? Was it compassion, or just a human response to a call of duty? Are those two just different ways of expressing the same idea? My observations of life suggested it was the latter. Was this the first time I had experienced compassion from my fellow humans, or was it just the first time I had felt it?

I was confused. I walked away from the church that day no longer able to pretend there was a God; I needed to *know*. It did not matter if some members of the congregation were faking their belief; I needed to know for myself that there was some kind of power beyond me. Pretending was beginning to cost too much, it was causing too much emotional panic-stricken stress.

Richard was taken to the hospital for overnight observation. When I picked him up the next day one side of his face had turned dark blue, but that bruise cleared over the next couple of days. We had been very lucky. Some would call it blessed.

One thing I was growing to appreciate was that due to the constant social and spiritual handicaps in my life, everyone was too busy to share their time for even the simplest reasons. Casual conversation was a foreign concept in my childhood and I had developed no conversational skills. Now as an adult I felt I could not discuss my chaotic life with God because I had been told that He already knew everything. I concluded he must be very busy and believed God was unavailable as a source of contact or a resource of comfort, even in times of emergencies.

My understanding of the church's impact on my life grew, and my new awareness was taking me farther and farther back in my memories. In my earlier years, I had been conditioned to lean on the teachings of the church. As I grew older I began to try to distance myself from a God that I did not know, and to distance myself from the church where I felt I did not fit or belong. However, as I gained awareness, my takeaway was that the difference between real saints and phony saints was that authentic saints knew their divine purpose.

I now realize one can become spiritually fit regardless of one's surroundings. At that time, though, as a young adult, all I knew was that I lacked knowledge on so many levels. I was not trying to be anything special; I just wanted to be able to get up every day and be okay with living my life. My panic seemed to be soul-deep.

Several weeks later I was seated in the basement of the church on a Saturday evening. The charismatic pastor was the facilitator that evening. There were maybe sixty women or more seated at the nine long tables joined in the shape of a wide square. I sat there with my "I dare you" mindset turned on to keep me company. I was still hoping for some old-fashioned miracle, as Emily Dickinson mentions in one of her poems. I had lost the battle of not drinking, but I continued attending church; I didn't know what else to do.

I am not sure what the study topic was that night, but my ears perked up when he asked, "What is forgiveness?"

"It's a release," I stammered ever so softly; I almost didn't hear myself.

The facilitator turned toward me briefly, then matter-of-factly whirled carefully around the opposite way until he had faced all four directions of his audience, repeating what I had said. "She's right," he reiterated with gusto, "you're saying, 'release me!'" Then he said, "The Holy Spirit told her to say that."

I was somewhat unnerved by the Holy Spirit statement. When the conference ended, I quickly left. I did not have any intentions to return, ever. I did not appreciate others imposing their views of holiness upon me. Being the center of attention was just too much. I did not appreciate a comment of mine being so powerful. I resented the pastor including me and the Holy Spirit in the same sentence. I knew absolutely nothing about sacred language, although I had heard the terms "Holy Spirit" and "Holy Ghost" all my life.

If I was going to be accused of speaking from inspiration, I wanted to understand my own brand of Holy Spirit experiences with facts, graphs, and details. At least that's how I felt that Saturday night at the church. Although, it was a good, short, and powerful dialogue with the pastor, it was probably the first time I had ever spoken aloud in public. Giving correct answers was not my typical mode of operation. Hearing the words, "You're saying, 'release me'" had been awkward and foreign for me. Why, the experience had frightened me dreadfully! Unsure if it had been the setting, the Holy Spirit statement, the public speaking, or the correct answer that frightened me most, I fled the room as quickly as I could.

Blurting out wrong answers was my custom. Given my lack of education and absence of much knowledge, I could hardly help getting things wrong, but I could never remember correctly answering questions in a setting of that magnitude. I was unprepared to be right or even to hear myself utter that three-word sentence.

If the pastor had been assertive and asked me to expound on what I had said, I would have been totally perplexed. I did not know why I had so readily uttered the words, "It's a release." I was completely puzzled by the words that tumbled from my lips. I had heard misinformed people speak regarding spirituality most of my life, but blaming anyone else was not my intention. As a matter of course, I blamed myself and my personal inadequacy.

I desperately wanted to know what being awakened required. How did it happen? Suppose I had missed my wake-up call. Had I missed other wake-up calls? Was it possible I had missed hearing the preachers' messages on Steps, Stages, and Processes of having a Born Again Awakening experience when I had sat cat-napping in the pews so many times?

From my outer appearance, no one knew my level of quiet desperation, discontent, boredom, and fear, for it was all so well hidden. No one knew how I struggled night and day, searching for any kind of a faith encounter – whether the size of a grain of mustard seed, or whatever - my misplaced hope, and my disbelief in God. I spent most of my time trying to hide my unsolvable issues, which did not leave any time for healing. I am not sure where I got the message to hide, pretend to be small, and cover your fears. What I should have been doing instead was discovering my genuine self-worth. After I left home, I became accustomed to dressing for victory; never mind that I had absolutely nowhere to go. Inwardly, I was a compendium of embarrassment, anxiety, and incompetence. Dressing up my outsides did nothing to activate the drastic change I needed within. I desperately longed for an inward transformation.

I learned to camouflage myself by changing my fashion look. I bought clothes from Macy's, Jones, and the Goodwill, pretty much in that order. I made great efforts to make sure my makeup was flawless most of the time, even at the local Laundromat. My hairstyles had to "represent" since I was a beautician, even if I wasn't currently working in a shop. In all of my brokenness, my hair had to be re-styled differently every single day, sometimes twice a day. My two children were well dressed and physically well cared for. Nobody knew how messed up I was on the inside.

I was in church one Sunday afternoon, minding my own business, walking through the dining hall. I just wanted to be in a healthy safe environment while I was waiting for evening service to begin. My plethora of social anxieties was driving me crazier than any one person ought to have to bear. I was trying to hold onto my church commitment. I did not want to go home between services. As I was walking and reading a paperback book, suddenly someone snatched the book right out of my hand over my head. My head and eyes followed the rising book, moving up and away from me in slow motion. It was the same charismatic pastor I had encountered before. He quickly closed the book and studied the front cover: *How to Win Friends and Influence People*, by Dale Carnegie. He returned my book without even an apologetic gesture and walked away. I kept walking back and forth while reading, like a pacing panther.

I understood that this was the pastor's church. I was trying to save my shattered and broken self. I instantly wondered if the great commission had changed for the church, which is to tell the good news of healing and hope, and demonstrate acts of health and wholeness, not of animosity and hatred. I had learned one thing from my early life of hard knocks: I have some control over just how difficult life can be based on the choices I made. He was a renowned pastor with a great congregation. He lit up the pulpit when he spoke and energized his congregation. I was stunned that I held no animosity toward the pastor's disrespectful act. I was amazed that his behavior did not further bruise my already broken and injured spirit.

As I look back on that experience, I see a "Daniel in the lion's den" moment. At that moment, I felt protected from his disrespectful act. There is a thin line between living your talk and walking your walk. I knew that in theory but, not in practice. As my book was being lifted over my head, it helped me to see and feel big insults through smaller emotional window panes. I was learning how to not let some cruel indignities affect my new self-discovery journey.

Still later, I found a small amount of relief by rededicating my life to God at the regular Sunday Morning Services and the Wednesday Night Prayer Meetings. A young lad of twelve years old would usually sing "Just as I Am" so angelically during the altar call, I felt moved to go to the altar every single time. After too many erratic times walking to and from the altar, the tall, charismatic pastor made an announcement from the pulpit during a Wednesday Night Service. He said, "You do not have to rededicate your life every time an altar call is made!" He might as well have called me out by my name. All of the mid-week regulars knew he was referencing me. For most people, that would have been a profoundly embarrassing moment, but I instantly knew he did not understand how humiliating it was to rise and walk back and forth on those days. I would have a long talk with myself, but obviously I was not listening. The minute the music began my actions were unstoppable. I was unsure if it was the young lad's voice, the piano, the organ or all three. I was in too much inner discomfort to internalize the unwitting insult from the preacher's remarks. I was also too focused on trying to find relief for my soul's pain. I hurt so badly, and it was not the kind of pain that one made a doctor's appointment for unless there was such a thing as a Soul Doctor.

I thought that's what Jesus was – a soul doctor. Perhaps my fault lay in not knowing for sure. What I know for sure is that some types of pain cannot be healed with money or medicine. The kind of agony and disgrace I was experiencing required something special, but I knew not what brand of special at the time. The pastor did me a favor. He let me know that the altar call was not what I needed.

I needed an answer, sooner rather than later. I was close to taking matters into my own hands. The preacher did not know I felt safe and protected from my overbearing mental thoughts each time I walked down the aisle. I never felt anything once at the altar. It was clear to me that I needed to embrace a generic God or continue to battle with my own nonbelief; the choice was mine. Both ideas seemed rather disrespectful somehow. I could not go on in limbo between the two perceptions "there is or there isn't."

One Sunday when I could no longer stay in my self-contained spiritual quest and debate, I purchased a bottle of Ripple at the liquor store not far from the church. It was an inexpensive wine that came out during the seventies. The too-sweet elixir had completed its popularity cruise by the early eighties. I believe Ripple was the new Wild Irish Rose. I guess its mission was to separate the "Winettes" from the "Winos." It allowed underprivileged hosts to have dinner parties and serve red or pagan pink wine without their bank account balances measuring the pinch.

I drank a swallow or two of the sweeter than sweet elixir. The tangy syrup was too sweet for me to swallow fast. I replaced the colorful cap on the chilled green glass bottle, then placed the still chilled bottle back into its brown paper bag. It was my plan to save some for later, sort of an after-church spirit treat.

Once I parked the car, I proceeded on into the church. I walked down the lengthy sidewalk, then up the three or four wide church steps. The minute I entered the foyer I began to mumble noisily, "There is no God, there is no God," I repeated this announcement maybe three or four times as began to sink down toward the soft, light brown carpet. I was still in the main foyer, which isolated the commotion and kept the noise out of the church sanctuary on the other side of the two swinging double doors.

One of the familiar ushers was the greeter that Sunday. She caught me as I was sinking to the floor. I am not sure why I was trying to kneel in the foyer; perhaps it was because I felt I had been forbidden to meet at the altar during the service.

I seemed to have been sinking to rise no more, as it says in the old spiritual hymn, "Love Lifted Me." The usher was whispering with a kind-hearted voice over and over, "Do not say that!" I continued ranting the four words. I had haphazardly rehearsed the words in my mind many times while closed in the back of the old, dark, truck beds. Someone else was trying to help hold me up toward the end. It was like my equilibrium was gone.

I was not sure if I was trying to surrender to or from the exhausting, relentless, battle of denial I had lived in and believed I would die in.

I continued to repeat, "There is no God," and with every faint breath I could muster, it seemed that life was leaving me.

The compassionate sister continued to repeat her words over and over. "Think it, just don't say it," she finally instructed. I was losing my strength to breathe every time I uttered my denial of God.

I was amazed by how easy it was to honor her request. I was able to stop verbalizing the denial almost immediately. I did not come to believe in God at that moment, but in that moment, the need to deny ceased. I could not believe the urge just vanished, but my thoughts were instantly altered as if I *had* been at the altar. I had kneeled at altars many times before in many different churches, but on that particular day, finally, I believe I was truly blessed, for the God I did not understand stepped in and helped me.

I had just endured the most dehumanizing experience in my twenty-six years of living. The second the request had been made and honored, it felt as if I had inhaled a new gasp of fresh air. Once I was physically and mentally stable, I walked back to my car, too mortified to allow myself to ponder on what had just taken place back at the church. As soon as I was safely away from the scene and sitting quietly in my car, I made a conscious decision to move to Albuquerque, New Mexico. That would fix everything, I thought. The meltdown had been too much. I drove back home, perplexed, wondering why I drank before going church. I'd always had unpleasant results when I drank, whether it was one swallow or as much as I could tolerate.

I had learned at age seventeen that if I wanted to drink alcohol I could only drink beer. The pathetic episode in the church foyer caused me to recommit, again, to drinking only beer. The feeling of self-defeat that Sunday morning seemed to be of an intensity in a class all its own. I was no stranger to feelings of defeat or powerlessness, but that day it was the ultimate feeling of human mortification. That experience was like no other in my memory. I had not dressed in my Sunday best that morning, I had been too exhausted to care. I had gone to the church and travelled to and from the altar just as the old hymn suggested. I came to Jesus just as I was: weary, worn, and sad.

When I returned home I was not sure what to do with myself. I felt as if I had embarrassed myself one too many times, for the umpteenth time, again. I had believed I would drink the Ripple and sit quietly throughout the beautiful angelic service. My nightmare of a life was continuing to find deeper and deeper levels of hidden embarrassment, hurt, and disgust. I still did not know why.

On one hand, I did not fit anywhere—not in my past or present. On the other hand, I wanted to try harder to look for answers, such as how to learn to be more tolerant, and how to like, or maybe even love myself. I wanted to learn how to stop revisiting my past; it was over. I wanted desperately to let go and move on with my life. I wanted to spend my roaring, roaming, energy discovering and developing new skills for life and experiencing true living. But, I was stuck in my icy numb mental pain. I had no idea what new emotional skills would look or feel like. I could not stop blaming, whining, or crying. Sobbing was the only language of communication that had any meaning to me. I did not know how to discard what was not working. It was hard to figure out what worked or what could or would be changed to stop the relentless, deep-seated pain and confusion.

I wondered how long I would continue to repeat old behaviors and ideas. It seemed as if my brokenness had grown to be a part of me and had become inseparable.

Chapter 10 - Silent Hope: 1975

My unproductive and restless pattern of perpetually relocating had already taken me to and from a large number of residences within Kansas City, Missouri. With any shred of common sense so clearly out of my control, this time I decided to relocate across the river to Kansas City, Kansas. This escape lasted three years. It appeared my misdirected instincts were bomb-rushing my steps into an all-consuming, obnoxious world of drinking, thinking, and numbly existing.

I did not know what the answers were for my life or my drinking. But I knew I had to find a better way to deal with both. During that time my children were the only significant reason I continued to strive for the betterment of my life. Marvin Gaye was singing "Save the Children." I seriously believed it was time to save Leona. It seemed that I had been lost and abandoned for far too long. My mind seemed to beckon me to keep searching for some means to develop a healthier and happier way of living, despite the continual bouts of defeat and disgust.

I had tried to learn how to love my siblings and I had tried to learn to love my parents. I concluded we were all too damaged to support each other. I had tried to love myself with all of my imperfections, but I could not for the life of me figure out where or how to begin the process of turning my mindless actions around.

As I returned to my little ground-level apartment after the great Ripple meltdown, I made a conscious decision to relocate to Albuquerque, New Mexico. I wanted to run far away from the Ripple Crime Scene and the hundreds of other failed, awkward attempts at trying to recreate my life.

I had quit my office assistant position the previous week. I had felt so uncomfortable showing up for three hundred and sixty-four days. One of the many habits that bothered me most was my co-workers refusing to stop saying, "Good Morning," to me. It felt insincere and awkward, and tremendously uncomfortable. It disturbed me greatly every time I forced myself to answer. I was quite withdrawn, to say the least. My co-workers continued to be their natural hospitable selves, but I did not have the mental capacity to reciprocate their hospitality. My tolerance lasted three hundred and sixty-four days, minus weekends.

On most Mondays, I had gone across the street to the Katz Drug Store for a hot breakfast. My anxiety would not allow me to eat on the weekends. I only had an appetite every three days. I looked forward to Fridays on the one hand, and at the same time I hated them. Weekends interrupted my ongoing struggle for stability with holding employment. It was always so hard to return to the same job on Mondays. Eventually, I decided that finding another job was better then returning to the old one. I suppose, considering my history, that decision was inevitable.

Whenever I became too exhausted from the repeated struggles to fit in and belong on a daily basis, and I just could not make it another day, then I just got up from my desk, gave a scribbled note to my supervisor, and asked that he give the note to the department manager. Once I exited the elevator, I walked out of the building, stepped into the breezy, sunny weather, and felt the embrace of liberation again. I caught the bus home. I never returned for my last paycheck or my personal items. I repeated this pattern more times than I can count.

This time I had made a mental and verbal commitment to remain on the job for a year. I wanted the negative behaviors and thoughts to stop. I managed to stay employed three hundred and sixty-four days. I could not will myself to make the three-hundred-and-sixty-fifth day. I had worn a different outfit every single day, which helped. I was already frustrated with my entry-level typing and office skills. There was a pizza establishment on the first floor of the fourteen-story building where I worked. This place also served beer. I conned myself into believing I could have pizza without the beer. Somewhere in the eleventh month of my employment I had begun to have pizza and beer for lunch. I would return to my desk knowing full well that the beer had not been a good idea. I was not the greatest typist in general; when I drank, the results were even worse. The keys on the electric typewriter would not obey my intent to produce flawless documents. Most of the managers drank their lunch and bragged about it, why not I? My concession to drink appeased my grave feelings of inadequacy.

With every move, I would either transport my personal items to the next place by car or I would leave them behind. This time, I would place my household items in storage. All I wanted was enough money to start over one more time in a different state. Invariably, I would find another job to carry out my plan.

When I decided to move to Albuquerque, though, instead of looking for a new job to fund the move, I applied for welfare to get enough money to purchase bus tickets, even though I had too much anxiety to wait thirty days for a welfare check. A couple of days later, I received a letter from the welfare office stating I was not eligible for assistance. Even though my life history was overflowing with one living disaster after another, somehow the welfare news cheered me a bit. At least it stirred my depression and anxiety somewhat differently. Handouts were not for me, and I had known that for a very long time. I fell back on my old pattern and found a job and worked four weeks, just long enough to make enough money to leave town again.

It was a Sunday evening when I began to gather my belongings from upstairs and downstairs and pile them all in my living room. I had become the kind of person who felt disturbed if I was not busy all of the time. Rapidly every room in the apartment was empty except one. I had pushed and pulled five rooms of furniture into my living room. I wrestled the mattresses and placed them at the base of the mushrooming pile. I dismantled three bed frames and placed the parts on or around the pile. I methodically made trip after trip to the pile. I felt alive.

I removed the legs from the kitchen table and added them to the pile, cleared all of the clothes from each closet, boxed up all the small items from the bedrooms, bathroom, and kitchen. I begin to dismantle my living room end tables. I pushed the living room chairs toward the pile. I disconnected the washer and dryer and left them sitting in the small laundry room, not too far from the living room. I unplugged the refrigerator to be defrosted and cleaned later. I had my own appliance dolly because of all of the moving I did. I realized much later in life that relocating was a form of entertainment for me.

It was exceptionally difficult for me to remain still. Somewhere along my journey I realized silence and stillness posed deep threats of both absolute terror and boredom for me. I was bored by nature anyway; more boredom felt just too unsettling. Other than going to church, the few times I was allowed to go to school were the only times I had been allowed or required to sit still. It was not difficult to sit still at school because the teachers always kept us busy learning something new; sitting still at work was a real challenge.

Further packing and shuffling continued into the wee hours of Monday morning. I stopped at six a.m. to begin to get the children ready for school. Richard had learned to run across the backyards to his first-grade class. I stood at the backdoor watching him disappear over the hills, out of sight. I walked my daughter, Secret, to her daycare center several blocks away, and then returned to my small apartment.

I had made arrangements for my brother to come over with his truck on Monday. The kids were gone, and everything had been placed in the living room for easy loading. I looked at the cone-shaped pile. I was exhausted. I climbed up to the top of the heap of mattresses, stretched out, and drifted into a nap. I was hopeful that a new start was going to save me one more time. My patterns of failure were becoming unbearable, to say the least. I felt so empty within, it was unnerving. But I was not sure what it was I felt or what to do about my uncomfortable feelings of nothingness.

During my restful slumber up on top of the heaping, stacked pile, I must have heard something with my inner ear. I sat straight up with a quick jerk to gain my bearings. I was disturbed that something had awakened me, and I knew not what. I climbed down carefully, as if I was on a steep hill. When my feet landed on the floor I was facing toward the back door in the kitchen.

Although the front door was closer to the pile when I came down, I was already facing the back door. I headed in that direction. As I walked forward, I noticed I had not secured the safety chain in the groove, but the deadbolt lock was locked.

Sleep had always been hard for me to come by since I'd left home eight years earlier. This time I had been relaxed and thinking about my plans to relocate when I had fallen asleep. I still did not know what had startled me.

I snapped open the bolt and turned the knob with a vengeance. I furiously jerked open the door in my state of agitation. There stood a slender, tall, fair-skinned African American male, maybe in his mid-twenties. He looked about six feet tall. He had a screwdriver in one hand, still in motion from whatever he was trying to pry off the door. What I had possibly heard was him trying to quietly open the screen door. I wasn't sure. The screwdriver was still wedged between the door frame and the stop molding.

When I yanked the door open, it startled him. He did an abrupt about-face turn and just walked away. I was still irritated that I had been disturbed. Those brief moments of rest had been the finest I had ever known. I relocked the screen door and the kitchen door and walked back to the steep, tall pile. I carefully scrambled back up the pile and waited for sleep to return. Before I could drift back off to sleep, I heard a knock on the front door. I quickly sat up again. I struggled back down the pile, stumbled, and staggered toward the front door. It was my brother, ready to help me load the steep pile onto his truck, piece by piece.

To me, it seemed there had been some divine protection earlier. I had not felt the least bit of fear or panic during the entire time I faced the intruder. I was more concerned about my inability to feel real danger. Why hadn't I been afraid of the man? Why hadn't his intentions spooked me even in the least? Had I experienced so much pain and suffering that I had lost my ability to respond appropriately when in danger? Or did I secretly want to choose death over life? I had always believed my fight or flight reflex response would kick in as a "plan B" but in this case neither response had been activated.

Still, I was unwilling to believe that my plight could not change. No one had modeled better living for me, yet I instinctively wanted what seemed better. I had seen plenty of possible alternatives from observing others, from reading, and from TV and radio and magazines; I knew other people were functioning better than I was, and I wanted to do what they were doing. My past was dictating my future and I seemed to not be able to do anything about it. Most of my everyday acquaintances were unhappy, depressed, poverty stricken, or dependent upon their employment to give them a sense of self-worth. I wanted contentment, peace of mind, and hope. Finally, I recognized the essential desire for change had not filtered into facing my everyday boring circumstances. I wanted to change but I did not want the discontent that sometimes goes with the process of change. What I've since learned is I can't have one without the other. I had prayed beggar's prayers, I had played "if only" games. Guilt and fear had preyed upon my mind nonstop and I was tired. I felt that I was in some sort of pre-contemplation cocoon waiting for the right time, place, or person to assist me.

So much of my time had been spent protecting my useless, day-to-day, vision-less drama. I was apparently incapable of looking at my unpleasant truths. I needed mental and emotional energy to change my perception. My outlook on life was riddled with uncertainty, swarming with fear, and jam-packed with uneasiness. It was not a secret to me that I was missing tremendous opportunities to take control of my life. I was just not sure how or when to seize healthy moments. My frustrations were not small. I could not make sense of where or how to start making changes. It felt like my heart and mind had abandoned me. I was experiencing a great deal of anxiety trying to learn how to maintain employment. In a fit of desperation, I enrolled in junior college to complete my basic educational requirements.

I went back to school hoping that earning my certificate would bring me some confidence. I hoped gaining self-assurance would help to make me feel better, even a small fraction better. When I received my General Educational Development Certificate in 1974, I was extremely disappointed. It didn't bring the satisfaction I had been seeking. Many years later I gained the understanding that the certificate was just a representation that I had finally achieved the most basic skill level. I had met just the essential, elementary requirements. To me that had not felt like *real* progress because it meant I was still nowhere near where I wanted to be. I had much more work to do. My struggle toward finding tools of real change and growth was nowhere near being over

I developed a new coping strategy, mostly by default: I would work as many days or weeks as I could, then quit and enroll in some business school course for another six months. I completed one course after another, always between jobs. Still, although I had hoped these small achievements would help me feel some degree of accomplishment, they did not, and I regularly agonized over my lack of progress. I worried about everything and never felt secure. I had no idea what would make me feel safe, free, and whole. I was worried that I would never know what real love felt like.

I had left home wondering if love was real, and, if it was real, how would I know? If I had children, would I have the capacity to love them? I sincerely worried about this, since I was not sure how to love myself. Would I raise them loveless, the way my parents had raised me? I left home wondering how I would ever be able to learn how to forgive with such a heavy, cold, heart of stone as mine. I had left home hoping the worst of my life was behind me. It was hard to find a way to measure past worst and present worst as I walked through life's daily ups and downs.

After tripping over many stumbling blocks, I came upon a set of nine small books entitled *Nine Fruits of the Spirit* by Robert Strand. After reading each of the small books, I began a self-study on how each of the spiritual gifts was applicable to enrich my life. I used the books as a study series in my morning meditation to learn more about joy, peace, self-control, gentleness, love, faithfulness, patience, goodness, and kindness. There was no doubt that developing the nine attributes was part of developing success. I love Valorie Burton's definition of success in her book, *Successful Women Think Differently:* "Success is living your life's purpose and embracing resilience and joy as you do." I found it to be my truth that once I began to understand the cycle of forgiveness, my attitude of resisting change became one of the greatest challenges for me. Once I surrendered to my nothingness and not knowing how to save myself, a flicker of hope was born. I began to have hope and laughter from a place of comfort which had once been completely out of reach. It seemed to me that I had missed so much personal and professional development. I wondered if I could ever catch up. I was now preoccupied with racing my way through life with the determination to catch up. I zoomed through one catastrophe after another in my search for purpose. Relocating kept me preoccupied with appearing busy. I had thought if I kept moving fast enough, no one could accuse me of not trying to accept my past or failing to move on.

Worrying about what I thought others were thinking was what I did with perfect perfection. Moving was my first step in trying to get my life right. Truth be told, finally I realized I had played the first step to utter distraction and I still had no idea what the other steps were for becoming stable and successful. However, I learned much later that what I had been searching for was acceptance, resilience, and emotional peace. When all was said and done, I was at last in a place, mentally and emotionally, where I could start to work toward reform and restoration; I had found my acceptance, resilience, and emotional peace.

First, though, I had to find a way to overcome my daunting past. I had hit rock-bottom and now I had to find a path out of the darkness. I had two children, and I was too weak from the long fight for my own internal survival to be able to effectively fight for their health and well-being. I knew I had to do something, or my family would be no more. When I began my nine-step meditation practice, my son was seven and in the second grade; My daughter was three and in Head Start. They were both doing well. I, on the other hand, was a total discombobulated basket case. I saw no way to improve my life, but I felt I must at least try. I needed so much growth and change. I knew I had to start somewhere, so I started with how I looked. I focused on something I knew I was already good at and made sure I was dressed well every day, broken hearted and all. My children seemed to have all of their physical needs met, but I missed not having any emotional ties to share with them. I was spiritually starved of human validation. Every day the strength came, despite what I felt, to try to be the best mother I could. I cried every day from dealing with all my unnamable fears, but somehow those tears helped me to find the will to persist in seeking workable tools to improve my life. I continued to hold one dead-end job after another until I had saved enough money to make another move. I lived in Kansas City, Kansas, until September 1975, when it was time to go start over somewhere else, again.

Chapter 11 - **Divine Faith: 1975**

After relocating to Albuquerque, New Mexico September 1976. I was optimistic and pessimistic about my future. I found employment during my first week. That job lasted for four months. I was doing well until the foreman insisted I have a drink at the company Christmas party. I mouthed the words *I don't believe I can drink,* and then I took the drink bait again one more time.

In Albuquerque, fortune teller businesses were a presence on every corner, like clubs in the Midwest during the 70s. After a disingenuous crystal ball chat, the neighborhood fortune teller just led me right back to the problem at the end of her outlandish prediction. The pseudo-psychic woman softly instructed me to drink warm wine as part of her prescribed remedy. As she said this, I remember thinking to myself, *I believe that's part of the problem.* Everyone seemed to think drinking was the cure-all for pain and problems. I was getting more and more desperate for peace of mind and was receiving more suggestions that a drink of this or that would do the trick.

I continued searching for fragments of hope to bolster my elusive and flickering determination. My outlook on life was getting dimmer and dimmer. I enrolled in a data entry program and kept trying not to drink. I had awakened the drink beast at the Christmas party, and it was fully in charge now. I found thoughts of not drinking repulsive, even though thinking of drinking kept me too preoccupied to think of little else. These conflicting thoughts of drinking and avoiding drinking were both tormenting and patronizing to say the least, and they hacked away at my already raw nerves. My mind was definitely tired.

I had met an African American woman in one of my data entry classes. She was studying the teachings of Buddhism and began sharing with me what she was learning. The unkindness of previous church folks had taken its toll on my weary, neglected soul, so I was leery of going the religion route again, but I cautiously began to attend meetings with her several nights a week. The Buddhists I met were very wonderful people. I did not experience the kind of cruelty I had encountered in Christian communities. We would chant, "nam-myohorenge-kyo." I would chant as long as I could; for five or ten minutes of the session. I am not sure how long the sessions lasted, but five minutes was too long for my restless anxiety span at the time. We began by chanting while kneeling. I would soon lie down on the floor and have a peaceful nap. Between the bells ringing and the chanting, I could not see the point. I was not finding enlightenment or anything else. At least it provided me a peaceful rest. I purchased their Chinese scroll, still searching for answers. One of the Buddhist leaders explained that if I looked into the scroll as a window, I could see my future." I looked, gazed, and stared; I could not see what they saw. I knew that chanting could work; it just did not work for me.

Eventually, I concluded that a place of comfort has no limits on where and how it can manifest. In trying to find or establish windows of hope, it was suggested that I should seek, and peace would be found. It was also suggested that my search for growth would always be a work in progress, whether in serving or being served.

As I was taking a walk one day during the time of the Buddhist experience, overwhelming despondency washed over me. As I surrendered to it with bitter despair, suddenly in my mind I heard these gentle, soft words: *The extent to which you are hurting right now is the extent to which one day you will feel joy*! For one brief second, I felt as if I had been showered with genuine joy. It was a marvelous contrast to my profound misery at the time.

The promise of those words was refreshing. The unexpected moment of joy lifted my spirit, but as quickly as the compassionate, energizing thought had come, the joyous energy disappeared again. That brief glimpse into my future was so profound that my pain actually paused for that moment in time. I wanted to be content with that small splash of hope, but my overwhelming anxiety kept me from basking in the glimmer of peace.

The joy had quickened my spirit with a shadowy tease of hope while I continued to struggle with my multiple emotionally blinding challenges.

Many dead-end jobs and business schools later, I was still short on marketable skills. Disillusioned, I left New Mexico and returned to Kansas City, Missouri, still trying to find something, anything, that would make me stop relocating, job hopping, and soul searching. Much later I understood the meaning of "a work in progress," but that concept certainly applied to my time in Albuquerque.

"Work in progress" could also be called "the process," and I was definitely working my way through "the process." I had lost my Texas Instruments job in New Mexico because of a need to drink. This losing and finding, hoping and failing, crying and trying, was beginning to frighten me. I feared that one day I would not care that I had tried my best and all of my trying had not meaningfully paid off well. Was I destined to live my entire life at the bottom of the ladder of satisfaction and success? Was it possible to be a perpetual failure and still survive? I did not want to accept this pattern as inevitable.

I returned back to Kansas City in mid-June 1976. I lived with my younger sister, Pauline, for a brief period, while I tried to figure out my next plan of action.

I had no idea what to do with my mess of a life. My chaotic lifestyle was the result of constant emotional swings between depression and downright dejection. My challenges were plentiful and never of the jovial type. The lingering grief that had plagued me from childhood was old, but still new. This insatiable, nearly blood-thirsty lust for order in my life also seemed old and new at the same time. In contrast, the impulsive, impromptu drinking was new. Death seemed near and getting steadily nearer. In my mind I was screaming, "But I've never truly lived!!" When was my happily-ever-after experience going to begin, in heaven perhaps?

One morning as I was lying in bed at my sister's home in Kansas City, Missouri, I was stirred to call the operator. I moved quickly from the bed to her upstairs kitchen. I did not have any idea what I'd say to the operator once I dialed, yet I proceeded up the basement stairs almost eagerly.

I was exhausted and filled with an intense sense of hopelessness. I was sober in my body, but not sober-minded. Finally, after reaching the last of the nine steps, I stood straight, took a deep breath, and marched toward the phone which hung on the southwest corner wall. I moved as if I had rehearsed the act. Lifting the receiver, I dialed "O" with my right index finger. As I waited, the operator's voice said, "Southwestern Bell, how may I help you?"

Words escaped from my mouth without my permission: "If a person thinks they have a drinking problem, is there a doctor that can help them?" I waited for her to say, "No there isn't, or not at this time!" Instead the operator answered, "Yes!" and proceeded to give me the information I needed.

This was a turning point in my life even though I was not ready for the "yes" answer I had just received. I was absolutely stunned, but relieved at the same time. For me, hearing the word "yes" was somehow enchanting and endearing to my heart and my mind. Up until that moment in my life, I had been too traumatized to be easily surprised by much of anything. Now, I was stirred, energized, for the first time; I had received another "yes" on my side from yet another stranger. Now I was speechless, without a doubt.

That "yes" reply was the first real surprise in my twenty-nine years of living. I listened intently. In just a very few seconds, the operator had provided me with the name of a doctor and a phone number. I thanked her for the information and placed the receiver back in its cradle. I walked from my sister's kitchen back down to my bedroom in her basement. I kept wondering what had made me, out of the clear blue, decide to call and ask for information about how to overcome my drinking? And where had that well-organized question come from?

Moving forward through internal and external devastation, befuddled madness, and muddled confusion was and had been stressful forever; it seemed like eons. "If a person thinks they have a drinking problem, is there a doctor that can help them?" I kept repeating the question. I never associated drinking alcohol with the medical profession, and it was unbelievable to hear 'yes' to the question once I had made the call. Even while I was speaking to the operator, I was pondering why I did not want to imply that I wanted the information for me. Was it a secret to me in some twisted way?

Every drinker I knew loved drinking and they all became giddy when they drank. It seemed like they were experiencing a Happy Hour event every time. Booze was always treated like the guest of honor for them. My experience with the implied guest of honor; booze, was not like that at all. Whether I tried to live my life with alcohol or without, it had always been one pure living hell. I had believed I could live with the hell of alcohol. I had hoped alcohol would even fix the chaos my life presented, and maybe even allow me to fix my other brands of chaos in the process. I had tried single-handedly to combat the stronghold of alcohol over my life. I found the whole ordeal peculiar as it was happening, but I could not defy nor deny that something out of the ordinary was happening with my life that would one day, someday, be for my good.

Up to that point in my life, I had not had any serious thoughts about needing help around my drinking. However, I did have thousands, possibly millions, of fleeting, echoing thoughts daily, weekly, monthly, and yearly that something was wrong – that my preoccupation of thinking about drinking all day long – was maybe not normal. Still, I was absolutely sure that drinking was not the primary problem, maybe not even a problem at all.

Drinking was still relatively new in my life, and I believed the actual problem was my lack of problem solving skills. I was sure that my inability to map out workable strategies for my life had caused me to start drinking. I had learned to survive amidst ongoing difficulties and had made a fine art of skating around and around, manipulating myriad stumbling blocks, frequently moving in circles where others were doing the same.

My life until then certainly seemed devoid of purpose, empty of healthy relationships, and without a healthy bond to myself, healthy family ties, healthy emotional or spiritual development, without financial wisdom, without successful educational advancement, without meaningful long-term employment, and without the understanding of how to live an effective solution-based lifestyle. I was having trouble forgiving others, with no concept of forgiving myself. I was having trouble just accepting things as they were. With all of that missing, it's no surprise that I found it impossible to move on to greater accomplishments. I was having trouble leaving those things behind me and pressing on to a decent higher calling. More importantly, I could not for the life of me move forward mentally, physically, or spiritually. It was as if I was trapped in a holding cell of self-produced chaos without a release date in sight.

I kept thinking, "Someone is going to pay for the hell I've been through, and the current hell I am going through." I could not get past blaming my parents. To me, it seemed obviously their fault. They were the ones who had set the ball of misery, bitterness, hate, shame, and guilt in motion. I figured they needed to be the ones to fix the ongoing mess with a simple apology, as if that would cure it!

The next day after the phone call I'd made from my sister's kitchen, I made a visit to the address of the doctor's office the operator had given me. I spoke to the doctor. I answered a lot of questions. When I stepped outside of the doctor's office that day it was half past noon. The sun warmly embraced my face with tenderness. It felt like the warmth of the fall sun was a great part of my support team. That feeling, like the feeling of joy that I had experienced earlier, was fleeting. Before many minutes had passed, I began to wonder, "How can I take back the information I had just volunteered to the doctor? What nerve of me!"

By talking with the doctor, I had shared my well-guarded secrets with another human being. Why did I disclose my top secrets about my drinking and thinking to the doctor? I thought those secrets were to be carried to my grave. But if I learned nothing else from that conversation, I learned that I would have to assist myself in getting up and out of the gutter by acknowledging my own flaws, faults, and failures. After I had spoken with the doctor I felt that I had blackmailed myself. I found myself unmercifully upset by the realization of the great torments I would have to go through in exposing my challenges to someone besides myself.

I began to obsessively think, "I have got to fix whatever I just shared with the doctor in his office. I have never told a soul, not anyone, that I couldn't be a good mother, I couldn't hold a decent job, I could not stop relocating from place to place, I could not laugh, I could not play, I could not hold my head up, I couldn't stop hating, and neither could I love. I had never told a soul I could not let go of my past. I could not stop dreaming the same dreams over and over. I couldn't stop screaming when I spoke to my children. I began to repeat myself, I could not stop thinking about drinking, I could not love myself, and I could not stop being angry with God.

Something within me sensed I would never get the courage to speak these particular words again, but I also had not wanted to stop the unpleasant truths as they rushed from my mouth. The act of disclosing, admitting my problems to someone else, was an entirely new and different experience. Later in my life, as I searched for answers to my plethora of dilemmas, I learned the precise names for my regular behaviors: *fear, insanity*, and *self-pity*. I later diagnosed myself as having Schizophrenic, Bi-Polar, and Maniac depressive behaviors.

Learning these concepts and applying these labels to my own situation did not instantly stop my ongoing victim party of crazed misery. Whenever I began to experience some sort of emotional or mental discomfort, I would almost immediately begin to rehearse the words, "Do thyself no harm." I did not know how to stop running from my brokenness and I feared I that had violated some moral code.

It was like my inner craziness was fighting back, trying to protect itself from being eradicated. This happened repeatedly, most frequently when I tried to come to terms with my chronic but unspoken need for love and acceptance. I knew I had not the capacity to love my children, yet I also knew I was supposed to love them. Somewhere deep within, I wanted to give them what I did not get as a small child. I knew I had desperately missed being loved, even though I had no idea what constituted love. I could not tell who I was the angriest with, my parents, God, or myself.

Even though I could not control the circumstances of my birth, or the behavior of my parents, I felt that I should be able to avoid hurting my children the way I had been hurt, but then my mind would argue back at me, "I was a girl, for crying out loud, with a trashy upbringing." Those words haunted me with every heartbeat. I found the thoughts and the experience difficult to live with and difficult to let go. I wondered if the thoughts would ever leave me.

I talked incessantly and hysterically about the family business to anyone and everyone, whether they wanted to listen or not.

I finally learned just recently from Iyanla Vanzant that I had become addicted to telling my version of the story. It was over, but I could not let go of the physical and mental tragedies which had occurred. I didn't know how to stop the regret without closing the door on the entire experience at the same time. I was not sure if it was appropriate to tell my childhood truth concerning my parents' employment. I was embarrassed to think about the family business experience, let alone speak of it, yet the hauling experience lay immovable in my psyche. If it wasn't going to go away, I at least wanted desperately to learn from the experience; I wanted freedom from my past. I spoke of my predicament to total strangers, family members, and co-workers, to anyone who would listen. When I was not rehearsing my dissatisfaction to others, I retold the story to myself, *ad infinitum.* I could not stop myself from talking and thinking about the disgraceful experiences I had lived through between ages six and sixteen. I had hoped the old trashy memories would just lose their power and divorce themselves from me. So many other cross-my-heart-and-hope-to-die memories had done just that, had faded from my memory; I hoped the trash hauling memories would just leave, not with a bang or even a swoosh, but by gradually deleting themselves over time without leaving even a trace of evidence that the horrible events had ever actually taken place.

During my meeting with the drinking doctor, when I finished crying, whining, and talking between gasping breaths, the doctor said, "I can't tell you if you are an alcoholic or not, but they have some meetings you can attend if you are. They may let you in." I was without understanding of what else I needed to endure except what I had already withstood. The unfavorable upbringing and the guzzling of liquor had convinced me I had some problems that seemed unsolvable. The combination of those two big issues, regardless of any others, had persuaded me to believe that I had done my due diligence and that my search for a better way of life had merely brought on more confusion.

After speaking with the doctor and working myself into a state of hysterics, I thought, "I do not want to go any farther. I've had enough!" I quickly composed myself just in case I was not willing to give up drinking forever. The idea of never drinking again was more terrifying to me than any scary drunk or frightening sober moment had ever been!

The doctor gave me two options. There was a group which met across the street from his office and there was another group down in the inner city. At some point during the conversation I had stopped listening because I had grown uncomfortable and was ready to leave. I was sure I had not heard any of what the doctor had said. Whatever he'd said could not possibly apply to me, I thought. The doctor spoke of his sliding pay scale for the visit. Because I was unemployed and without an income, he charged me no fee, and so it was that I left the doctor's office with a sense of integrity and dignity I had never previously known.

Still, I was upset that I had succumbed to the impulsive plot of dialing "O" for the operator, speaking with the operator and not hanging up, calling the doctor the next day to make an appointment, and keeping the appointment. What had I been thinking? My state of mind was ruffled worse than it was before I had stumbled up the steps at my sister's house and made the call.

Five days later my kids and I were boarding a Greyhound bus headed for Texas. Once I found a seat, I looked out the window at the uniformed driver standing outside, waiting for last-minute arrivals. For some reason the logo of the sighthound on the side of another greyhound bus reminded me of my inability to stop running from one place to another. I briefly wondered if I would ever slow down and get my life together. Tears welled up in my eyes. I blinked my eyelids a couple of times, took a deep breath, and my tears refused to fall. Instead the tears withdrew and I felt strong again. Getting my life together simply meant living in one place longer than a few weeks or months for starters, having reliable transportation, being employed, and learning to live in the now. It also simply meant not being afraid, having the confidence to accept what I could not change, and not running from the things I needed to accept. I still lacked the ability to slow down and plant my life on solid ground and allow myself to bloom.

I had stayed in Kansas City for about one week after leaving New Mexico, and now I was running away to Lubbock, Texas. I was trying to escape my insistent, yawning desire to find love, hope, and comfort. Answers to my unstable and shiftless life were difficult for me to find. I knew I yearned for a better way of living. I yearned for peace, I yearned for contentment. I figured if my family could not love me as I believed I loved them, living in another state would make it not matter so much to me. Plus, what I had shared with the doctor still baffled the heck out of me. What I had shared had shaken me to my core that day and I still felt in total disarray four or five days later.

Chapter 12 - **Dancing with the Devil: 1976**

I arrived in the great state of Texas at dawn in early September 1976. It was a Sunday morning. Sundays had always been sad for me for as long as I could remember. I had expectations of Sundays as days to get closer to God for one reason or another, by sitting in church and lifting up praises or just having great heavenly dialogue with other people; otherwise I felt as if hell was winning. Sundays never quite lived up to my expectations.

I had been napping during the bus ride. I opened my eyes and peered out the window as the bumpy rhythm of the bus ended my nap. I noticed a small storefront garage as the bus slowly rolled toward the terminal in downtown Lubbock. It was an older style garage requiring someone to manually open the two doors, which then blocked the sidewalk until the car was driven inside and the doors were closed again. These were locked with a chain and padlock. But I noticed boards had also been nailed in various directions across the doors of the old, weather-beaten, once-upon-a-time-storefront meeting place.

Then I saw the letters AA painted at the top of the garage. I panicked, thinking *AA is everywhere!* Here I was, running from the conversation I'd had with the doctor back in Kansas City only a few days earlier, and now in my new town the first thing I run across is an AA location. The doctor had only discussed AA in passing, but for me even the lighthearted hints were too bothersome and unsettling. I had never heard of AA or even the word *alcoholic* before my visit to the doctor. Listening to him speak on the topic disturbed me, and I was not sure why.

What I knew for sure was that I was only twenty-nine and I was much too young to be stripped of my new cunning friend, alcohol. For some reason I assumed if you could not find God, then drinking was the next best substitute. I had tried to think of my multiple inner forms of chaos as "fun," but the entire conversation with the doctor had disturbed me greatly. I was not sure why the visit had affected me so. Guilt and remorse had always bothered me with their intensity, but I was rarely moved by anything else.

After my surprised recognition of the AA symbol, my eyes released the double As, and rapidly darted downward to the lower part of the garage. I was relieved when I realized the AA place was out of business. Thank God! I let go a deep sigh of heartfelt relief.

Something about AA was the main reason I had left Missouri this time. The doctor's conversation had left me feeling suspicious and confused. My outward composure, which was typically all I ever let anyone else see, was rattled. My inner composure – what I thought of as my self-contained spirit – was completely discombobulated. I did not know how to liberate myself from the experience or even how to keep from re-running the conversation in my head. I could not ignore the doctor's effortlessly implanted diagnosis and his simple suppositions. He had been well-trained to deliver his analysis in a way that would have an impact. "They might let you in," he had said, with an almost amused, nonchalant look. I did not know what to make of the expression on his face. I could make even less of what he had said. "Might?"

The bus pulled into the terminal. There was a hotel near the bus terminal. I spent the entire day there with the kids. They had made the trip with me on the bus, and I made sure they were safe and fed, but I was merely going through the motions. My thoughts were continually preoccupied by the AA idea and my conversation with the doctor. The next day I found a place for us to live and enrolled my son in school and my daughter in daycare. When the kids were settled, I started the familiar job hunting process. The walk to the employment office was quite lengthy from where I now lived. I realized I needed a car for any of the positions available. As I was leaving the agency, there were three or four African American males lingering outside on the steps of the office building.

I asked, "Where are the liquor stores?" realizing I had not seen any red neon signs flashing "Bud" or "Bar" during my long exhausting walk. One of the fellows, who could have received an award for his melodramatic performance said, "It's w-a-a-y over there," while flailing his arms and pointing both index fingers as if he was pointing a rifle. He was implying that Lubbock was a dry county, which I learned later that day.

Almost instantly the job became secondary; I knew I needed a car primarily to get to wherever "way over there" was. I thanked them and headed east. Walking back to my new home in the flats without a job seemed to take twice as long, and I was twice as sad. I had always felt lucky since I left home, but that day I briefly thought maybe my luck had played out. I could not hold my head up, even though I tried it then. I had always walked with my head down. I never knew why; it just seemed comfortable. Or maybe it made me feel less noticeable. I felt so undeserving. When I was younger, I had learned to count the cracks in the sidewalk to distract myself from what was going on around me. This day, even with the distractions, the sidewalk seemed longer than ever.

Just as I approached the top of Avenue C where I had now lived for two days, I looked down over the horizon. There appeared to be a junk yard down below. There were dozens and dozens of large, long, dark brown objects. As I made my way closer to the scene, I could see the deeply scorched and severely sun charred objects clearer; they were metro buses parked in the barnyard with sun burned tops. I turned and headed south toward the scene. It was the Lubbock Transit Company.

I walked in and saw no one. An older male voice came from somewhere in the back of the main office area. He had heard the cow bells on his door jangle when I'd entered the small, one-story building. "May I help you?" the male voice asked. The voice seemed to be getting closer to the front of the office where I stood waiting. "Hello? Are you hiring any female bus drivers?" I almost yelled in a voice of sheer desperation. It was a voice of confidence which had exploded with a sense of freedom. As terrified as I was to be in a new city again, there came this strong, strange voice from the same place within that told me every now and then that the stresses of life sometimes had value. I could sense the person speaking was coming closer while engaging in conversation, even though I did not see anyone right away. The manager of the company finally made his way to the front counter which separated the office from the entrance. He asked me a few questions, then handed me an application as if he'd known me all of my life. One of the questions he asked was whether I had ever driven any heavy equipment before. I weighed a whole whopping one hundred and twenty pounds.

"Yes!" I almost shouted again. He continued with his questions, and I then went into what I'm sure must have been an unbelievable spiel concerning my parents and their business.

It was the first time I'd spoken with genuine enthusiasm about the value of my childhood experiences. I actually felt energized as I was finding worth in the gatekeepers' attempts to make their business successful. Years of built-up animosity toward them quickly took a back seat for a minute or so.

I completed the application and handed it back to him. He said he would review it and check my references and give me a call. I left feeling hopeful that I had the job. About an hour or so later the phone rang; it was the man from the transit company. He asked if I could come in tomorrow for training. I was so excited by the opportunity that I shouted my response: "Yes! Yes!"

I arrived at work the next day with much anticipation to begin my training. To hear someone compliment me on any of my skills was new and different. I did not quite know how to say, "Thank you." I was back in the stressful situation of needing to exercise basic courtesy skills and I was very uncomfortable.

I learned early on that Lubbock was a dry county and I had already been free from drinking for a couple of days, so I was becoming agitated. The Sunday before my first day on the job, I began to think maybe I could speed-walk my route to speed up learning my job. I commenced to walk my route. I walked a few blocks and decided that was a bad idea. I returned home discouraged because I could not carry out my desired plan. Up to that point in my life I had always carried out whatever strategy I deemed important and this disappointment surprised me. For the first time in my life, my job was bigger than I had expected it to be.

Thus far, most of my behaviors and solutions encompassed spending many wretched hours drinking (which I had called fun). I had often consoled myself that when I reached my golden years I wanted to have a lot to reminisce about from my life. Even though I was still in my twenties, I had been on my own for over a decade and my life had not yet taken on even the smallest amount of true, purposeful meaning, certainly nothing to feel sentimental about.

After I received my first paycheck, I bought a hooptie and managed to make it to the liquor store, which became a regular routine. I would try to reason with myself to wait until the weekends to drink, but the pressures to perform effectively on my new job were too great to wait. Undue worry about my life and my performance on the job and continuous feelings of "woe is me" would set-in, and those feelings kept me great company.

I had made it through six months of mental games, moving time and again from asking myself during the day "Can I have just one drink?" to nonstop thinking, "Is it possible or impossible?" I was losing the battle in my own head and the battle with the actual drinking. I can't tell you how many times I was driving my bus after having had a drink or two or more before starting my shift. Thinking about the baffling possible/impossible question made me downright dizzy.

One day, as usual, I made my first early morning run and returned for my afternoon shift. While driving on one of the main busy boulevards, I could not figure out if I needed to slow down to make the upcoming right turn that was just up ahead a short distance. Should I pass up the turn and get back on track later? While this debate was racing around and around in my head in real time, I was fast approaching the intersection where I was to turn into a small residential neighborhood. I had to decide whether to turn or not to turn. I approached the corner without a solid decision – I couldn't decide if I was going too fast, or if I should slow down. Just before the turn, I was sure I could not make the turn safely without the bus turning over or colliding into the car waiting at the corner to turn onto the thoroughfare.

As I started swiftly turning the steering wheel, I waited for a solid bang or crashing sounds from somewhere. My window was open. I noticed a little boy standing up in the back of the exiting car between the passenger and driver's seat in the back of the car. The little boy screamed from the bottom of his lungs. Maybe that car was a convertible, I am not sure. After I did not hear a slam, bam, or bang, and realized that the bus was still right side up, I guided my vehicle on up the residential street, as if to say, "Wow I did that!" That's when I heard the voice again. It had been silent for a long time, but now it said, "You know you have a drinking problem. Do you want to kill someone too?"

Between my unyielding willfulness, my constant high level of anxiety, my fragile nerves, my constantly evolving marriage(s), my two children, more nickel and dime jobs than any one person ought to have experienced in so few years, and not being one iota closer to a God that I understood, I mentally screamed in my mind, "No! NO!" I could hardly bear up under the load of my various personal crosses, let alone deal with another thing that might cause harm to people other than myself. I decided I could not allow myself to accumulate any more liabilities on my ledger. I completed my route that day and turned in my uniforms the next day, completely uncertain of my next plan. I was already wounded, hurting, and filled with rage at all the difficulties and problems weighing me down. I did not want to place additional burdens on anyone else or myself if I could help it.

As I thought about what to do next, about how to find a way to move forward with my life and get a grip on my anxieties, one of the disquieting incidents that my memory would not let go of involved the late A.A. Allen and his tent revival events. We had attended one of his events back in 1959, and it was now 1977. As a young adult I'd developed the weekly habit of going to the library to check out books. In the beginning, I had argued with myself over what types of books would interest me since I had struggled to master reading and had no particular subjects that appealed to me. The committee in my head soon reconvened with a verdict, "Select books on any subject." My shame gremlins (a name I borrowed from Brené Brown's book, *Daring Greatly)* were apparently on my mental library committee. I must say the committee was right on point.

I trusted the committee. I trusted the gremlins. I did not trust me. I was obsessed with having opinions about everything, but I had not yet developed the ability to evaluate criteria, so I could consciously and intentionally make basic decisions. One week I checked out maybe four or five books from the Lubbock Library. I was not seriously interested in any of these books; I was just going through the motion of acting as if I were invested in the process again. After staring at them for a while, I decided the books needed to go back to the library, but between my chronic depression, the round trip I had walked to and from the library, and the scorching hot Texas sun, I could not will myself to return the books that day, although I wanted to.

Instead, for some reason, I began to frantically thumb through the books while still standing outside of my apartment door. I was so agitated that I just kept flipping pages, looking for I knew not what. The wind blew a small piece of paper from one of the books as I was flipping through page after page. A small ticket-sized piece of paper slowly fluttered to the ground – quite slowly – despite the breeze. I stooped to pick it up while holding the other books tightly in the cradle of my other arm.

It was a clumsy move, and I almost dropped the other books, but I managed to reclaim the loose scrap. It was an ancient yellowed news clipping. I later wondered why I didn't just let it go, but in the moment, I found I couldn't help myself. I began reading: "The late A. A. Allen…was found in a hotel room, dead." I quickly entered my small apartment and sat down. I was free of my depression for a second or so. It was like the sense of wonder I had held so many years earlier had returned for just a brief moment. For whatever reason, this time I was able to let the drama go that I had silently held within for so long.

I was freed that day from the plaguing, demonic thoughts that had held me in their grip for many years. I took a deep breath and finally let out a much overdue sigh of relief. I'd had no idea of the level of pent-up torment and pressure I had lived under for long. A tiny, aged newspaper story had set me free. I read it several times. The clipping had found me unexpectedly. It was a moment of genuine revelation, deliverance, and reconciliation. The minister back in Kansas had been right. I did not have to rededicate my life at the altar every week. Salvation could come to me anywhere, any time. I was standing outside my small apartment when I was set free that day. I debated whether I should turn around and carry the dull books back *now,* prior to looking through them. The thought of the books I had so hastily checked-out now bored me. After I read the news article, I received enough energy to wait at least until tomorrow to return the books.

I had been in Texas only eight months. Whatever I did not want to accept about my drinking eight months prior, I now knew my denial about my drinking was as great a danger as the actual drinking had ever been. Drinking was out to destroy me one way or the other, and my relentless denial had been making me not care. Those days were now over. And now I had to decide – again – what to do next.

In 1977, I learned I didn't have to relive past years. I had a choice, and ultimately it was up to me to want to c-h-a-n-g-e, to g-r-o-w, and to l-i-v-e, not necessarily in that order. I just had to learn to face the music, no matter the type, from Acadian to Zef. I had to learn how to deal with life some way, somehow. Therefore, I would have to figure out how to face life on life's terms with the help of others, including my Creator and myself.

I could not do battle with physical death, but I could strive to want to live, I could learn to respect others, and I could learn to love myself. I wanted to live with purpose, but I was not sure how to move into the lane of purpose. No one in my many circles had ever spoken of their discontent. I was well-acquainted with mine; discontent and I had been inseparable acquaintances since I was six years old. Now I was finally tired of being discontented with myself and my life.

In retrospect, some of the seemingly unforgiveable challenges that had been forced on me by my parents when I was younger had taught me how to survive. I had learned enough to keep on living, and now they gave me more power than the pain they caused me at the time. I had actually endured and survived. I had lived through and moved beyond circumstances that had once seemed utterly insurmountable.

To know that I can forgive gives me energy. I somehow understood that I had to let the ugly, unhealthy, evil, mean-spirited, unsuccessful events die. I heard or read somewhere that "the pain of the past only comes alive when emotional energy is given to it." I was not sure if this was true or not, but the statement made a believer out of me instantly by just my having made contact with the information. In 1963, Martin Luther King said something that resonated with me so much that I later adapted it to my own life: "We are determined to be free in 1963." This slogan had given me a personal sense of hope and harmony. Somebody else knew the troubles I'd seen and felt trapped by. Knowing that I was not alone had helped me feel more normal, more human somehow. I had lived in an inexplicable world of losses. I did not know how imprisoned I was until 1964, when I was thrust into the real world to begin my adult journey even though I was still just a child.

Sitting in different pews at church, exhausted and aimless, had become my time-out space as a young adult. Returning time and time again to Kansas City after long, emotional, reckless, uncharted journeys through various states and too many neighborhoods to count had worn me out. I was beyond tired, past exhaustion. I was ready to surrender to whatever could save me from my self-absorbed, meaningless existence. I was beginning to accept my fate, as it seemed no matter what steps I chose toward a better direction, it seemed I could not separate myself from the terror and abuse of my childhood. I wanted to change my outlook on life and learn how to embrace all that life had to offer me. I had seen some members back at the church in Kansas City, Kansas that were living a life I wanted. A life of peace, happiness, working side by side with others, and they seemed to enjoy their space and who they were. It appeared that they were connected to something greater than themselves. I knew I wanted that!

It was challenging to figure out which steps would lead me to where I desired to go, and which activities would produce positive results. I had no experience with good decision-making, or even any decision-making; life had always just happened to me. Now I was actively choosing my own direction, but it was still difficult to tell when one process was ending, and another was beginning. The only information I could easily understand and make use of turned out to be lesson plans created and presented to me in my dreams. During my waking hours, I could see no association between my conscious daily thoughts and the sporadic nighttime messages from the gentle inside voices in my head and heart. I also did not see any obvious signs of personal growth for many years.

When I was young, I had somehow learned to rely on instinct when my instincts were all I was capable of risking, believing, or trusting. Through my dreams, thoughts, and personal insights (i.e., the voices that kept speaking to me), I was guided slowly but surely to a place of authenticity and restoration.

My parents had abandoned and evicted me from the only life I had ever known, putting me in much distress. I was unsure of life and myself. I was afraid to trust me. By the time I was dismissed from the family business at age sixteen, my personal inner strength, my sense of personal empowerment, had shriveled to nothing, leaving me ill-equipped to fend for my weak, confused self. Lack of trust in myself had become a frightening roadblock to success in any daily activities. I couldn't even begin to think about abstract traits like self-efficacy, self-empathy, self-confidence, or self-motivation, let alone self-compassion. I had no sense of my own value, or any appreciation for any accomplishments I may have had in my early life. Instead, I embraced what I knew best: my feelings of failure. I remember hoping that someday I would have feelings of success, but at the time all I knew how to do was continue on my lonely journey, ready to meet disappointment around every corner. One thing I knew for sure: I knew I could not drink about the dilemmas I had to face, not if I wanted to keep myself and other people safe.

Looking back on it now, I know I had always moved from one neighborhood to another, but I seem to have picked up the pace around 1969. I was uncomfortable wherever I was and always felt the need to be somewhere else, at any cost. I was running away from everything and everyone. Discontentment had its way with my mind, my humanity, and my soul.

I can't say exactly when I had this particular dream, but it haunted me to utter distraction. I was always restless, even when I was asleep. During one particularly unsettled night, I had a dream about what seemed to be a possible intervention session. I was being asked a series of questions by someone I did not know. Some of the questions my anonymous interviewer asked me included: "Why does the need to drink seem so important to you so much of the time? When you're not drinking, why are you always thinking about drinking in some fixated way? When did this need to drink supersede all other basic needs?" I did not know the answers to any of the questions being thrown at me. I had questioned myself many times before about my drinking and its relentless pull on me. However, the questions the anonymous person was asking were originals. I must have wanted to ask myself the same questions prior to hearing them in my dream, for now I wanted to know the answers as well.

After that dream, my focus shifted to the point that I spent entire days obsessing about "this drinking thing." I thought about drinking, where and when to have a drink, how much to drink, what was too much, what happened last night before drinking, while drinking, or after drinking. Why did every aspect of my chaotic life seem boring except drinking? When did this new drinking sensation overtake my mind? When did I become the person who was filled with protests and denial about my problem? Why was it so hard to admit I was addicted? Why did I feel I had to give in to every last alcohol-loaded drinking demand? I could not turn off the intruding thoughts about alcohol from my first drink at seventeen to my last drink at thirty. I had not a clue how to get my life on a worthwhile track. The need to drink seemed to have eased its way in without warning, and now it was bullying my entire emotional committee. Drinking had become far too big a part of my life, putting me in demeaning situations, demanding all my attention, and turning me into something more like a demon than a human. I knew I needed to make changes, to sort out my shipwreck of a life. Where I had always been driven by anger and fear, I needed to be driven by something else, but I still did not know what that something else should be.

The steady allure of the drink had other ideas. I had trouble maintaining the energy to keep struggling to improve my life and break free of the constant summons of alcohol. It took all my determination to be continually seeking something better. To get better employment, I was enrolling in one business school after another. Taking care of my two precious children was a huge task for me no matter what else I was doing. I was also trying to develop elementary social skills so I could interact with other humans, and that was an overwhelming, daunting job, one that I could not hand off to someone else. Change was too slow in coming, and I was running out of resolve.

I found myself attending my first real non-church meeting. I was in a dream. Everyone was already there as the meeting began. In the dream meeting I was with several people trying to help me figure out what to do with my unsolved problems. An elderly male voice said ever so nonchalantly, "Maybe you will have to go to the little white house up on the hill where the people do not drink!"

Those words shocked me into a state of panic within the dream. I yelled, "Why me? Why would I need to go to a place where people are not drinking?" I finally bellowed, hollering until I was out of breath, "Why would I want to go to a place where people are not drinking?" The mere thought of not drinking was inwardly forbidden by some inner code, something I did not control. When did this happen? I had always believed I was drinking by choice. Yet now, in this dream, I finally saw that the power of choice had left me when I took my first drink in 1964.

"I cannot live without drinking!" I shouted to no one in particular. There were other faceless, nameless people in the dream intervention session; I wanted to make sure they heard me! I finally woke up, sat straight up in bed, and reviewed – in my head - the elements of the dream I had just interrupted. I got out of bed and walked to the kitchen and fetched a glass of water to calm myself. I never kept alcohol in the house. I didn't drink often enough in the beginning to feel the need to keep it on hand. As time went along, drinking helped me feel like I wanted to continue to live. Between 1964 and 1969, I still had some control over my drinking, but I had grown to *want* to drink; it made me feel better. By 1970, my use of alcohol had progressed from casual consumption to a driving need. Between 1970 to May 2, 1977, my only real inspiration for living came from drinking alcohol as often as possible. The need for drinking had become overpowering. The particulars of wanting it, obtaining it, drinking it, needing it, thinking about it; stumbling over close calls with danger because of it, the preoccupation of a one-track mind, all became the most important thing in my existence, all centered around "the drink."

Reminiscing about what happened last night, the night before, or even years ago preoccupied my mind. Finally, I noticed the increasing need to drink and think with each new sip. How would I busy myself to not think about drinking or actually not take a drink if the desire showed up? I didn't know. I was in a state of shock just thinking about living without drinking and what that entailed. I never dreamed that I could ignore one urge to drink, let alone hours, days, or weeks without the thought of drinking dominating my actions. I tried to remember when wanting to not think about drinking had become so powerfully, exhaustingly intolerable. Again, I had no idea.

Meditating about drinking, moment by moment, had been the one skill I'd perfected. When I was in my late teens, going to house parties and clubs kept my mind preoccupied and gave me a false sense of being busy between needless worries. It was my greatest pastime. After my kids came and I was the sole provider for three people, my trips to and from the liquor store to purchase alcohol made me feel like I was living. My social entertainment with my new friend, alcohol, was exciting. I would take mental trips with each sip. It was a sad, sad one woman party, with many soul filling songs playing on boom boxes, record players and the car stereo "Let's Get It On," by Marvin Gaye, spun on the turntable overtime.

In the end, my tolerance for life and living had become too hopeless to keep trying. Waking up in the morning was becoming too much of a hassle. How would I get through my routine of interminable seconds, minutes, and hours? Getting through one annoying twenty-four hour day was beyond bothersome. The "how" question would not dismiss itself. I lacked sufficient energy to survive even one day without drinking. There were not enough internal or external distractions, not enough things to do to, to keep me from being held captive within my own sense of boredom.

Thinking about getting through twenty-four hours a day without alcohol had become my daily distraction. The perplexing situation would not let my mind move beyond the thought of denying me even a swallow of alcohol. How would I get the first minutes of my day started? How would I forget the ugliness of life which had introduced itself to me thus far? Would I ever see the value in myself? Not knowing the answers to any of these questions and more made it safe to keep drinking, thinking, and processing my confusion as usual. I did not know this then, but I was waiting for my encouraging team players to show up and help me. Sometime much later, one day when I had grown tired of waiting for team members, I became my own first team player with God's help.

I had actually received an inner message from a small voice within, early in my teenage years. I was seventeen and had been attempting to add drinking to my life to alleviate the boring twenty-four hour shifts of living. Still fresh from the hauling business, my life had no purpose. This was not a dream; I was wide awake. As a matter of fact, I was walking along Brooklyn Avenue, still a teenager, still trying to get through one numb day after another. It was a command much like an ultimatum. It had been like a news flash interrupting a TV show already in progress.

The news was: "If you are going to drink, you are going to have to drink beer!" "Beer?" I shouted to no one in particular, again. "No! No! No!" I argued and shouted, still walking. I had many reasons against limiting my drinking to beer, but the main argument was that it was too time consuming. Needless to say, I was half a mile past livid! That was my first real resentment. Beer! I kept repeating it to myself all that day. In the end, however, I learned to love beer; I believe it was my first love. It did not have to be malt liquor, either, just ordinary beer was enough to keep me on some level of contented chaos.

Eventually, I got to the point where I would have willingly died for a drink of beer. I loved the taste, the smell, and the white froth. I finally lost interest in hard liquor, wine included, without any serious effort and with no real awareness; it just happened, but I loved beer.

Chapter 13 - **Home, at Last: 1977**

Eventually, my wondering and wandering began to disturb me. After all those years of erratic behavior and depression, I became so frustrated by my inability to make sense of my life that I began to search and research everything I could get my hands on to find some relief, some meaning. I inhaled information like air, and I learned a lot, but the double wide gap between receiving new information and being able to make use of it was huge and seemed useless. I realized I needed to find ways to soothe or slow down my thinking.

I had left Lubbock, Texas and arrived back in Kansas City, Missouri on, March 4, 1977 and brought with me a feeling of defeat and hopelessness. I was ready to just give up, but I couldn't; I had to keep going, if only for my kids. I *had* to find a way to function like a normal person.

I told myself that what had happened in Texas was a thing of the past. The living daylights had been scared out of me more than a few times during that short spell in Texas, and I kept reassuring myself that the near-fatal collision had not been that bad. Nobody had died, at least. Now that I was back in Kansas City, I realized that whatever I had not learned prior to the doctor's visit in 1976, I had unintentionally (and providentially) learned during my eight months in Texas. I could no longer pretend that my case was any different than any other case like it. I needed to quit lying to myself and get help to straighten out my life.

The truth, my truth, was that asking for help was scary, much too scary for a chronically frightened person like me. I knew my life was a mess, but I did not know what to do to make it better. I had no idea where to start or which direction to go to shift away from living dangerously close to disaster and toward living safely, happily, and with purpose. I was still lost, but now I could admit it, if only to myself. I started awkwardly, rationalizing and justifying my weaknesses to myself so they didn't seem so damning. I couldn't get myself to make a decision, to commit to making changes that still seemed highly unpleasant and nearly impossible.

Even though I saw many people living their lives with promise and order, I could not seem to find my own sense of purpose. I was slowly perishing without a vision for my life. It was difficult to want to create a better life for myself when I valued my own life so little. I *knew* that all the chaos I had been through and continued to go through would only get worse and likely lead to genuine tragedy if I did not find ways to change my situation, to learn to make better choices, to protect myself from myself.

When I had sat in the doctor's office just eight months earlier, I had omitted some facts when I told the doctor my story. Then, while I was in Texas, I found myself experiencing even more terrifying consequences due to my lack of self-control than I cared to admit. It was not pretty. The daunting episodes from day one in Texas had helped me to reach my own verdict. I could no longer dispute the truth I was facing. On May 2, 1977, a small, still, quiet voice reminded me of what the doctor had said: *You need to find the inner-city address you received from the doctor eight months ago.* This time, I obeyed. I had managed somehow to hold the address in my mind through all the reckless drama, trauma, and the steady flow of "I am not going to drink" broken resolutions back in Texas. The pretend limits I placed on myself had become less and less credible: "I am not going to drink until I get the children in school" gave way to "I am not going to drink until I find a place for us to live." Once I had found a place to live, my new limit was "I am not going to drink until I find a job." Once I found a job, then the goal became "I am not going to drink until I learn my route" and then "I am not going to drink on work days." When I started working a split shift during the week days, then it was, "I am going to drink only one beer before my afternoon shift begins."

I asked myself many times, "If you do not believe you have a drinking problem, why do you keep repeating 'I am not going to drink, until this or that?' What I now know was my rational mind wanted to be a part of my problem solving team.

I had returned to Kansas City after a long, emotional, and reckless journey through many temporary residences and three states. It seemed as if I'd gone through the entire experience blindfolded, running into depressing dead-ends and detours in quick succession. I was mentally and emotionally exhausted from living through all the near-misses, the dangerous events, the sleepless nights, the daily uncertainties, and my always present wish for someone to rescue me. I reassured myself constantly that I lacked the ability to save myself. It simply was not humanly possible. I was beginning to accept what I had been telling myself for many years, that no matter what corrective steps I took, I could not out-run, out-live, or separate myself from the traumatic, damaging experiences that had defined my early life, and now I was facing new dilemmas also seemingly beyond my control.

My rambling, racing thoughts would not give me a break, no matter how I fought to straighten out my life. I was obsessed with constantly rehashing, reliving, re-failing my string of deserted jobs and residences. The lies I told myself were for protection, but they were nonetheless illusions. Blaming eased the pain of failure somewhat, so I looked for someone or something to blame whenever possible. I wanted change, but I didn't know how to make change happen, and I could not for the life of me understand why God himself would not turn my troubled life around like zap! Surely, He knew I had endured more than my fair share of injustices and unfair treatment as a kid! Was that not enough? If God loved me, why would he not fix my life for me?

My intimacy with fear made it easy for me to ignore the reality that my problems were completely attributable to my poor decision-making and that God could not take responsibility for those decisions any more than anyone else could have done. As I child, I had no experience with decision-making; my life had been completely controlled by my parents. I bore no responsibility for their choices, but I also did not gain important life skills I needed so I could function well after I was dismissed from the family home. I spent the second sixteen years of my life learning lessons I should have had the opportunity to learn in the first sixteen years. Those second sixteen years of involuntary emotional and intellectual growth were nothing short of living in pure hell right here on earth. They were completely different from the first sixteen years of hell on earth, but they were still hell.

It was April 1977. I had settled in Kansas City, Missouri. I acquired a copy of the local Yellow Pages and called a series of companies until some employer hired me. I was not drinking that day. A day or so later, I drank again. That time, my new supervisor was to blame; not me, I told myself. She had suggested that I have a drink from the portable office bar left behind in the main reception area after an office event. I tried to quietly tell her (and myself) that I thought this was my problem. "No, I can't drink," I had mumbled under my breath.

But I did drink and was immediately driven to a psychotic state of mind which demanded that I quit. I was only fired once out of forty plus jobs. With all the others, I would just not show up, or if I showed up I would just abandon the job during the eight hour shift. A day or so after I quit that Kansas City job, I found myself sitting in a night club with three of my sisters. It was about eight o'clock in the evening. Where we were seated, I could feel the fresh, cool breeze from the open entrance behind my back. The band was playing loudly as they performed a jazzy number. Once our drinks were served, in my mind I heard the low distinct voice again: "You do not have a place to stay of your own, you do not have your own transportation, you do not have a job, and you've just spent your last money on a drink!" The snapshot those words conjured caused my mind and my actions to finally heed the call. The underlying message was clear and left no room for misinterpretation of its concise meaning. I even sensed a fed up and impatient tone from the messenger in my head.

Not having money was nothing new for me. I seemed to always have just enough financial means to get by, nothing extra. Between taking care of my children, changing jobs, and relocating, managing my finances was not on my immediate agenda. Besides, there was nothing to budget! I needed and wanted something greater than I could imagine. The statement from the messenger was very clear. I said to my sisters, "I am going to leave. I will see you all later." I walked away from the small table and out of the club, leaving the chilled, frosty glass of beer on the table in front of my empty chair. I was surprised the glass of beer did not beckon for me to come back. When I arrived at the place where I was temporarily staying, I replayed the events that had just happened. In my mind, I could hear my sisters saying, "There she goes with that trying to not drink again." I had been trying to not drink for thirteen years, ever since my first drink at age seventeen. No one else knew I became a different person when I drank. Even to this day my family refuses to believe I had a problem with drinking which demanded that I not touch a drop. The miracle happened when I stopped waiting for others to point out what I already knew so deeply.

The next morning, I acted upon a solution as a dare to myself. The information I had received from the doctor eight months earlier still seemed crystal clear, fresh, and specific. I had finally found a place to begin, hopefully a process that promised to change the course of my life. Having a physical address and other stabilizing supports in place was a sufficient start, it was my first feeling of hope higher than zero on a scale of zero to ten.

That night, I found more hope than I had felt in all my thirty previous years of living. Around eight p.m., roughly twenty-four hours after I had left the club the night before – I went to one of the addresses the doctor had suggested. I was very uncertain, and very nervous. I was sure my new-found hope would disappear at any moment, but I went anyway. That was May 3, 1977, more than forty- one years ago.

I found employment again, and this job lasted an unprecedented and unbelievable eighteen months. When that job ended, I then applied at the Division of Family Services and was hired. I was amazed! I did not want to drink. I wanted to keep my job and keep my life on a good path. I worked for DFS for the next six years, from 1979 through 1984. The longer I worked there, the more my hope and confidence grew.

My tiny, mustard seed-sized grain of hope and faith had grown and was thriving. I found my grains of hope in the least likely situations and places. I took on several part-time jobs along with my full-time position, just to develop the habit of showing up and being reliable. My faith was shaky, but my little bit of hope felt great! I had never felt such steady satisfaction before. It was like having something priceless, and the value of it continually renewed itself. I purchased my first home in 1980.

I began to look at my life from a different perspective. I was now a stable human being, a competent mother, and an understanding family member. I was putting my family's welfare first, and that meant not listening to my tainted, mixed-up ego. On a small scale, I had finally gained the wisdom to know the difference. I wanted to grow up and achieve greater self-awareness.

As much as I had learned in my journey along the new path, I still had no idea how to set about achieving my long-desired goals. I would continue to take two steps forward and run or slide backwards. It was almost as if I got some kind of pleasure from not making progress. It felt weird, odd, and unnatural to engineer a different outcome for my life than the one that had been laid out for me earlier. I had already spent a lot of time – years, in fact – making the same mistakes over and over and never learning from many of them. It was like I could not stop the counterproductive, sabotaging behaviors. I wrote many gratitude lists and self-help letters. I was even asked to mail one letter, but I never did. One thing I knew for sure was that it was going take more than a postage stamp and a little travel time to save me from myself. Over time, though, I learned to become grateful for my many small steps, forwards and backwards, to the left and to the right, in season and out of season, always maintaining a degree of hope that was unbelievable and surprising to me, given my circumstances.

As a kid, I had seen the huge gaps in comfort, confidence, and safety between an economically comfortable life and the hand-to-mouth existence that forces one to survive in an environment of scarcity. At that young age, I am not sure how I knew that I was being taught to think and act in self-defeating ways which would later need to be changed, but somehow I did know it, on a subconscious level at least. I did not know, however, the heartbreaking pain it would cause to surrender to the things I could not change.

Learning how to live differently was another story. It was not all bad, following the stepping stones leading toward learning how to live purposefully. The choice would be mine. To change or not to change, that would be the valid question whenever my life teachers appeared. I never imagined I would need to be one of my own steadfast teachers.

There were many street-smart teenagers for me to hang out with during my teenage years. It was strange to me to be around them, to watch them. I knew I wanted something more, something better and different than most of those kids in our neighborhood demonstrated. I was not fascinated by their actions at all, although

I paid close attention to them. I was a square, and I hated it. I found, though, that doing what they did, and acting like they acted, did not bring me the joy and comfort I was seeking. I needed something else. I found that something many years later, when I learned how to look inside myself for answers and for change. Learning how to be genuinely true to myself somehow turned out to be a great benefit. When I finally realized I had discovered what was missing, I felt overwhelming relief.

When I was young, I often wondered if we as children were being misused, misled, and hustled by our parents. It felt like that was happening, but I didn't have the thinking skills to fully understand the situation. By the age of nine or ten, my inner seeds of madness, anger, and rage had rooted enough to keep me anxious, obnoxious, and edgy. I grew protective, combative. I was ready to do battle with anyone and everyone, but I was also afraid to do anything. The inner frustrations and mania-level energy would only reveal themselves at home or when I was physically working in the hauling business.

Good morning, good night, thank you, let me help you, and please were priceless phrases, but they were never used in my childhood home. Gentle communications like these go a long way toward helping a person feel accepted, loved, needed, wanted. These sentiments were not expressed in my family. All outward signs suggested that my parents would have been just as happy with no children, or far fewer, except for their need to staff their hauling business.

Over the years, I have learned that many – probably most – people have endured unpleasant and unwanted experiences in their lives to varying degrees. Some people try to make sense of their lives by ignoring the negative, acting around it, or covering it up and pretending the bad things never happened to them. They just keep going. Other people speak of God's love but cannot explain what that is. Somehow, despite this lack of tangible proof, they manage to make the most of things – they learn how to cope based on faith. Others somehow turn their midnights of torment into days of merriment and move on despite the torment.

I desperately wanted to be one of these people. The pain for me was unstoppable, despite money, God, or medicine. I could not hide from it, and I could not cope with it. My recurring bouts of acute discontentment were most challenging. I would get the urge to run, to hide, to start over, and each time I seemed to need to go further than the last. When I began to relocate obsessively, one of my brothers – the humorous one – always volunteered to help me. He would load my furniture and my possessions into his pickup truck. "When do you want to move?" he would say. And just like that, I was moved to another location. I would set up camp until the next whim to escape hit me, and then I would call him to help me again, and he would say, "Where are you going to this time?"

The day I moved to New Mexico, we hauled five rooms of furniture to the U-Haul storage in Kansas City, Missouri, from Kansas City, Kansas. He never asked questions. He would cheerfully and carefully load up my belongings and help me to get the job done. He did this for me for years, right up until the time I left Kansas City, Kansas and moved to Seattle, and he was never judgmental or critical. His kindness was uncharacteristic for my family, and it helped me to accept him and all the rest of my siblings from a distance.

I was looking for more than I could explain to anyone, but somehow a little peace of mind would have sufficed. I could not control the chaos in my dreams when I was asleep or the disorder in my life when I was awake.

I had once traveled from Albuquerque, New Mexico to Kansas City, Missouri for a quick visit. My oldest brother invited me to play cards with his friends while I was in town. He always had a lot of card-playing friends. He was so proud of me that day for some reason, and I had no idea why. Dressed up on the outside, within I felt like a bona fide failure. It was difficult to pretend to understand acceptance, love, or care. "This is my sister," he'd said proudly to everyone around the table. I felt a twinge of acceptance. There were folks everywhere. I nodded and smiled incredulously. I had not expected acceptance, yet there it was. It seemed a tiny bit easier to smile that time. As he introduced me, I felt a million miles away from authentic comfort, if there was such a thing, but I began to want to know how that felt.

My brother sat next to me and helped me play my hand. I did not feel entitled to his demonstrative support. One thing I knew about myself was I could not concentrate. I could not follow what cards had or had not been played, and I couldn't get invested in the game. I found playing cards monotonous. The happiest moment for me while playing cards was when my partner and I lost; I was relieved. When my partner and I accidently won, I was not happy; that only meant I had to try to follow suit over again. "Playing" just for the sake of relaxation or human interaction was just too foreign to me.

I was still attempting to learn how to enjoy being employed and stay employed. I was still struggling to find more meaning in my life. I craved joy and needed to be self-supporting.

I found it too conflicting and difficult to connect with most of my siblings even after we'd all grown up and were on our own. I was determined to find a life of social, emotional, spiritual, occupational, intellectual, and physical wellness. I knew I wanted to be transformed into a fully mature and functional person. I did not know how to make that happen.

It took a very long time to figure it out, but my problem was I needed to learn how to learn, and learn how to apply what I learned in ways that would let me prosper and thrive. I was willing to learn. I was not sure where, or whom, or how to ask for help. I seemed to need a lot of information that I felt I should have already mastered.

What I did not understand was that I did not know what I did not know. It was conceptually too complicated to even think about. I certainly did not know how to act on it. I did not know the right questions to ask or the right people to ask. I kept expecting myself to resolve problems that were far too painful and for which I had no answers. The craziness, in lieu of finding and accepting sane solutions, continued to baffle me. I finally learned that for me, pain and discomfort were a part of the effective process of change. Moving forward, especially in the beginning, required faith in something greater than myself. I feared that my "greater" something just may have to be God, but I could not figure out how to accept God being a part of my reality. Although this kind of information surpassed my understanding at the time, today, God *is* a reality in my life!

The absence of problem-solving skills meant I was given the opportunity to fail, far too much opportunity. I was given so much opportunity to fail that I began to think my greatest success *was* failure. I was excellent at being a natural failure; I had trained for thirty years on how to fail and cling to that failure so tenaciously that I could not let go. It was like holding onto the anchor after dropping it over the side of the boat. I could not allow myself to succeed as long as I knew I would ultimately fail.

Somehow, I finally learned to be okay with my small, incremental successes and see them as achievements. The most crucial lesson for me was to learn that *everybody* fails throughout life. It's how we learn and grow. We learn what we did wrong and we try to do it better the next time. Once we have mastered one thing, we can't seem to help but push ourselves to try something else we don't know how to do, and so we start again with trying and failing and trying and failing, until we succeed, and become competent, and gain mastery. All of this came from the slowly developing knowledge and experience in my long and awkward journey of coming to believe, not just in myself, but in God as well. This is how my tiny grain of a mustard seed of faith evolved into something large and strong enough to sustain me, even in my most challenging moments of doubt.

Chapter 14 - **That's Good!**

If I had to summarize what happened to pull me out of the vicious cycle of despair I was caught in from 1947 to 1977, I would say I finally experienced a spiritual awakening in 1977. I was introduced to gratitude and humility in 1977. These two forces, combined to awaken my desire to grow and become teachable, and nurturing those desires placed me in a lineup to be coached by unique, expert teachers. I found my spiritual and emotional home.

These teachers, these mentors, have influenced me to develop a wellness tool box. My educators also taught me many other things. One of the many insights they shared is how to allow their experiences to aid and guide me into my own journey to find a faith that works for me in both fair and foul situations.

In early 1977, while I was still in Texas, I received a spiritual message that I needed to take care of an unfinished soul matter which involved forgiveness. It was humility that had nudged me in 1976 and suggested I finally take a look at my compelling desire to drink alcohol. And, on May 3, 1977, it was humility that helped me to make a decision to diagnose myself so I could get on with my life, and somewhere in that diagnosis was a message in: "Grow up and Live!" Humility helped me to accept the things I could not change. I could not change that I was addicted to alcohol. I could not change that I had experienced repeated and desperate failures in my life. I could not change that I had lived through some terrible things and that I had been deprived of essentials like basic education, food, clothing, and love. But I *could* change how I responded to those things. I could choose to live differently. I could define my life for myself, instead of having my life define me. I could find a purpose and use that purpose to provide myself with the incentive to change the things about myself that were hurting me. I learned that having new understanding offers me a choice to surrender daily.

I heard a dear friend of mine from California gave me a definition of humility long before I was graced with an understanding of the word. "Humility is a rising in spirit," he said. That reminds me of the saying "You shall know the truth and the truth shall set you free."[5] I did not know what "a rising in spirit" meant at the time. But the idea set me free nonetheless.

Humility seems to show up in an unsuspecting place within, and its presence cannot be ignored. Its message of soul delivery is profound, soft, quiet, and gentle. It seems to whisper, "Let's try again." Its whisper seems to come without warning. Its irresistible pull leads with its own subtle power. Humility has many qualities; one is that it nurtures darkness and offers a friendlier, lighter horizon. Humility speaks many truths, and one is, "It's okay to try." Humility is not aggressive, but it is firm. Humility beckoned me to lift up my head one day, after I'd walked with a bowed-down head for over twenty-four years. Humility embraced me with a spirit of self-awareness, a spirit of protection, as if saying, "I've got your back."

Humility helped me climb above my fears and allowed me to wipe away my mental and physical tears of regret. Humility increased my mental and physical tears of joy. It has been nothing but humility that has increased my faith.

When I was at one critical turning point in my life, that moment was brought into focus for me by the unexpected arrival of humility. The thought came to me unexpectedly: "Just maybe, this might work. After all, what do I have to lose?" I was amazed when I internalized the thought, as if the words were being spoken by my coach, only at that time, I did not have a specific coach. Just maybe it was genuine humility which somehow had broken me away from the fragmented and fraudulent spirits which had held me captive to my horrific past.

---

[5] I know this is a bible verse, **John 8:32** "Then you will know the truth, and the truth will set you free," but it had to be a truism long before it became a scripture.

Now humility allows me to view my past simply as a stepping stone path to prepare me for making yesterday's experiences a foundation for greater, more fulfilling tomorrows. Perhaps the sharp words I'd heard in Texas - "Do you want to kill someone too?" - perhaps they got my full attention in a way that I could not comprehend otherwise. My life was zooming right past me as I waited for someone to help me.

I needed so much reform it was unbelievable. I blamed myself for my lack of wholehearted participation in learning to establish goals in my earlier years. In truth, though, I was too busy trying to fit in and belong to my environment. I believe an individual is generally a byproduct of their environment, whether that environment is healthy or unhealthy. Until one is willing to learn how to detach, and more importantly, to understand why detachment is necessary, they remain a victim of their circumstance. In my case, I remained a victim far longer than I like to admit.

I needed to put away my childish illusions and take responsibility for myself; I needed to learn to live a self-determining life. I needed to quit playing adult games while thinking and acting like a child. I could not stop the age factor. I could, however, take the actions needed to grow toward genuine maturity. I needed to grow up to know that there was a way to treat human beings without causing hurt, harm, and constant self-loathing. I somehow knew that the fundamental answers lay first in learning how to stop the pain, yet I knew no one who dared to mention their pain. Somewhere along my journey I convinced myself that I was the only one so uncomfortable. It hurt to think that perhaps I was not the only one hurting. Believing I was the only harmed one allowed me to justify finding destructive ways to block the pain. My beliefs had allowed me to use my pain as an excuse and had allowed me to take my excuses too far. I looked for relief by any means necessary, such as drinking, whether it was productive or not.

As unhealthy as learning to blame had become, the mixed-up part for me was that I had an automatic list of circumstances and people to blame each day. I was never without the list and I was never on the list myself for thirty long years. My life was always somebody else's fault. I finally reasoned that the blame was somewhere outside of me for some years and within me for other years. Because of the lack of healthy practices around me as a little kid, blame had become a compulsory band-aid that kept me alive until I was equipped with the tools to move past blame and into actively working toward productive, happy, joyful living.

Yes, I had encountered overwhelming grief and had survived the initial shock of it somehow, and I had found someone to blame for it. I had faced my own deficiencies in both basic education and life skills, and struggled to accept my many truths. I carried unresolved fears and pain, and I had moved from residence to residence, to the next block, to the same block, around the corner, up the street, across the river; back and forth, to and from one town after another. I kept searching for a way to escape the relentless, searing hurt that I had not yet learned how to face.

I had taken one business course after another in the 70s. I had wondered over the years if my parents were oblivious to the damage caused by their abusive, exploitive, and deprivation-based lifestyle, or if they simply did not care. It may have gone unnoticed both within our community and within their professional circles, but it caused great harm to me (and, I suspect, to my siblings also).

I had traveled back and forth on too many anti-social avenues of shame, blame, hate, and loneliness. I made many wrong and occasionally right turns, hoping to arrive at Serenity Boulevard somehow, someday. Eventually I did get there. However, in 1970, I was still right where I had started as a wounded, misguided child and young teenager.

I have searched through my life over and over, and I still come up short of finding any influential person who might have crossed my path early on. On the other hand, several people appeared when I was thirty years or older, when I had finally learned how to listen, humbly, to my inner voice and how to recognize kindness and compassion when it came my way.

During my journey toward taking charge of my own self-improvement, my unhealthy self-talk was loud and clear: "You don't belong here. Why do you continue to try? What's the use? And who cares anyway?" Resigning, giving up, and fleeing from place, pain, and difficulties were automatic responses; these coping mechanisms were familiar and the only remedies I knew. They fueled me with instant gratification. I finally learned that these were built-in messages from a place of self-pity where I had found a haven. Self-pitying behaviors and thoughts gave me some kind of superficially rewarding feeling. I had to learn to recognize those superficial rewards for what they were before I could change my thinking enough to understand that there were other, better rewards to be had from genuine growth and change, and that I was just as worthy and could have those rewards the same as anybody else.

As a child, I always drew strength from listening to the late Reverend C.L. Franklin's sermons from one of my LP's as I sat in my place of comfort[6] by the window upstairs on Brooklyn Street. One quote intrigued me: "It does not take anything to go backwards; you can kind of just drift backwards. But it requires effort to go forwards, and to be persistent." Even though I was not exactly sure how to utilize the words of the statement at the time, the language of that declaration always gave me energy. It became my pillar in my foundation of light. The words still are a part of my wellness tool box to this day.

I moved to Albuquerque, and later to Texas, with the innocent belief that life would be better for me. It was difficult to tell if I was fleeing from something or searching for something. I always felt as if I were in solitary confinement. By the third or fourth day on a new job, I felt just as trapped as I had on the job before. I had held many factory positions which I was overqualified for. The monotony of the conveyor-belt jobs and standing still drove me absolutely nuts. I was not used to standing still. I wanted to learn how to stand still and not be driven mad by the boredom of it. I wondered if it was possible. Returning to school and completing four business courses had not increased my confidence at all.

When I became employed with the Division of Family Services and held that position for six years, that experience of staying in one job for an extended period launched a new phase of growth

---

[6] The spot by the window was more than my favorite spot; it was the place in the house where I went to try to gather my thoughts and emotions, to try to make sense of things. It was the one place I felt relatively safe.

and self-awareness for me. The longer I stayed in the job, the more confident I became that I *could* stay in a job.

Once I felt more secure with maintaining employment, I wanted to give some attention to my wayward emotions.

I had not the faintest idea of what faith looked or felt like. I did believe I was supposed to find faith in church. So, I attended many churches. It may be that true faith is and can be found in the church, but that is not my faith story at all. I am not sure where I got the notion that attending church equaled developing faith somehow. My faith came to me differently and built up slowly; it started by learning how to remain employed, and from achieving other frustrating milestones successfully.

It had been exceptionally challenging to live within an environment where humility, compassion, and self-control were treated like unwelcomed intruders rather than as beloved guests that were always welcomed on arrival. You know, the type of guest who is greeted with "Come on in and make yourself at home," and "Let me have your coat and hat!" To develop these healthy behaviors that were once foreign to me, I thought it would help to see someone demonstrating these traits naturally. I wanted to see a hard copy lesson plan of growth procedures, but I found out sometimes it's difficult to tell or share the steps, stages, and processes of change. What I saw was originality in action.

I still remember how energized I felt when the baritone voice of Martin Luther King Jr., called out to the nation on our black-and-white Magnavox console TV in 1963. As a sixteen-year-old, I saw, felt, and believed in hope for the first time in my life. I paced around the living room slowly, wishing I could go to Washington, DC. I wanted to attend the March! It was my first powerful desire. I watched as people carrying their packed lunches boarded the buses, headed for DC. Oh, how I wished I could join them!

Later that year, before I was evicted from the family home, I remember looking out the upstairs window, wondering how to feel genuine and worthy, how to assert myself in ways that would be meaningful and productive. The inclination to give up was sometimes overwhelming. The battles between negative and positive spiritual states has been terribly challenging for me.

Despite my long journey of therapeutic recovery from all sorts of personal and professional failings, ultimately, I have survived.

My many peaks and valleys have not been easy to conquer, but I have learned, finally, to accept my challenges.

The perilous journey of my spiritual quest, shifting gradually toward an authentic birth of surrender to my own growth process, has taught me numerous lessons.

I recently heard an interview with one of the Seattle Seahawks players after a game. When asked how the team had managed to pull off a difficult win, the player said: "We were built to finish, and that's what we did." I could easily relate to what he was saying and found myself musing as I listened to the short interview. I, too, felt beaten and defeated physically, emotionally, and mentally, but I was not finished. I just had hang onto the belief that there truly was a therapeutic restoration waiting for me, if only I would survive long enough for it to happen.

Still, survival wasn't easy: the kind of hurt, disgust, and humiliation I felt daily kept me from feeling optimistic, even though hope and faith were simmering away somewhere so deep I couldn't always feel them. I sensed I would need a touch of the hem of His garment in some symbolic way. I needed an old-fashioned miracle. I was still fighting a serious internal battle with my own "truths."

In the beginning I was sure I did not have the courage it would take to outlive the pain I had already endured. When I was told that to experience the pleasantries of life I would be required to go through more hurt, hell, and pain, I could not fathom this being my truth or the truth. My options for recovery looked mighty bleak. I had to continue to secretly ask an invisible God in the obscure midnight hours for help with my mental pain. My reality was that I believed with every fiber of my being that God had let me down and let me down hard! Yet my pain and grief were so great and unbearable that I compulsively sought His presence day and night. More importantly, I had to beg for strength and courage to find my way if it was meant for me to outgrow the bitter, miserable circumstances of my life.

In the beginning, I had hoped and searched for a spiritual way of life within the Christian Faith, but I had lost that natural willingness to search or believe by the time I was ten years old. I was unwilling to continue to hope that there was something either outside of me or within me that would guide me, teach me, and support me, something that would give me confirmation that I was indeed on the right path. Much later, I could not imagine that there was something that could help me to endure my failures, misfortunes, and steady disappointments. My lack of growth as a child in Missouri was frightening. It is no surprise that I reached the conclusion that I was unwanted, beat-up, and useless. It took a very long time, but a faint willingness to believe finally returned in 1977.

Later, I became willing to call on whatever God was out there or within me. I needed help from somewhere or someone to hear, change, forgive, and comfort me. Little by little, I began to imagine increasing my efforts to gain a greater understanding of different belief pathways that could calm the raging sea of hate and confusion which still lay within me. I researched anything and everything that would or could show me a possible path to peace. I felt I just had to find The Comforter everyone kept referring to. I was frequently told that God was not lost, so I did not need to find Him. I would think sarcastically to myself, "I've heard that saying one thousand times too many; and regardless, of who is or isn't lost, how do I get from being religiously *mislaid* to spiritually *established*?" I had searched high and low, and I was not any closer to a spiritual understanding than I had been in 1953; it was now in the late 80s.

What I learned during those thirty-plus years is that there are steps, stages, and processes to achieving lasting personal self-leadership goals. Some of those steps are spiritual in nature; some are more social. What I've come to understand is the struggles I was having were not special or unique; they are universal. I also learned it is my responsibility to find healthy solutions that work on my behalf, as others find the solutions that work for them. I was searching for more self-confidence; with that growing contentment came a small degree of peace of mind.

I was still looking for easy answers that would allow me to make the shift from a life of complexity and turmoil to a simpler, more peaceful existence. During the time I was in New Mexico, I met some Buddhist leaders who taught locally at evening meetings. They said I would find answers for my life if I looked with focus into the scroll. I knew I had always been gullible, but I purchased the scroll anyway and began to work with it with a sense of desperation mixed with a tiny flicker of hope. With my high degree of anxiety, this chanting experience just added to the trouble, confusion, and frustration I felt, partly because I was incapable of sitting or standing in one position for hours and hours, or for even thirty minutes.

Another reason the practice seemed a lost cause for me was that the scroll was written in Chinese. I already had so many problems of poor adjustment, I was ill-prepared to focus on any one feature of my case load of problems. I was at the time struggling with using proper English when speaking or writing; it was almost comical, even in my emotional discomfort. Trying to interpret Chinese writing and symbols on top of all the mental chaos at least added an ounce of humor to the situation. "What dedication," I thought, "trying to find an understanding of my life with a foreign language and no interpreter!"

The elegant scroll certainly portrayed an exquisite backdrop for my studies, as if it could deliver peace despite what seemed to me to be my superficial reality. It also had a look of keen, sacred radiance about it. The scroll mirrored back a spray of isolated peace, yet in the space between the Chinese characters and my eyes, there seemed to be a veil of upheaval blocking the tranquil scene. I knew the teachings of Buddhism worked, they just did not work for me. While attending these meetings in New Mexico, I chanted "nam-myoho-rengekyo" and drifted into peaceful naps each time. I am grateful for those short experiences. However, I did not find the strength, faith, or understanding I had hoped to find.

When I first left home, I learned to scream, shout, and complain at great length to my mother by phone. My confusion and disgust became my habitual state of mind. When I would phone my mother, I believe I was trying to learn how to live within the reality of who I had become as a product of my childhood experiences and environment. I needed my parents' help until I could help myself.

My mother never hung up or tried to make sense of what I was going through. Looking back, I am sure she did not know what the voice of crazy sounded like when spoken aloud. She had done an excellent job of stuffing her own heinous discomfort into silence. Eventually I concluded that this was just the way of things. On the other hand, unlike my mother, I did not have any fear of expressing my discomfort, frustration, or dismay. When I was finally exhausted from my telephone rants, I'd hang up and wait for the next time. Sometimes my phone outbursts happened multiple times per day; sometimes I would go as many as thirty, sixty, or even ninety days between melt-downs. It was as if I was detoxing from the shock of my insane childhood.

One day my mother said, almost in passing, "You need to quit drinking." I was about twenty-four years old. For a split second, in my mind, I retorted, "When I was a child, for whatever reason, you chose to ignore me and insisted that I work religiously in the family business. Now I am on my own trying to figure out how to live a decent life, and you finally want to tell me what to do or not do. Well, it's too late." I never said this to her out loud, but my resentments toward her increased after this conversation. I did not know how much I resented her until that moment. I was appalled at her suggestion. That conversation left me fuming, but it also left me wondering why I took such offense at her simple and concerned statement. This was my second known resentment. I had begun to drink at the least little thing. "The gall of her."

From the speedy, choppy chattering in my mind, I became aware of how many different weaknesses or vulnerabilities I was trying to conceal. Although I was intentionally trying to cover up my inability to effectively communicate, new levels of self-doubt always crept in after every attempt. It simply hurt somewhere in the pit of my stomach after each conversation I had with others. I continued to stay on the path of change, though; what I wanted was much greater than what I had. What I wanted was to communicate without so much intense anxiety. From so many moments of truth and feelings of inadequacy, I learned I had two options: remain the same or accept the discomfort of change. I chose the latter. This choice may not always have been conscious, but it was consistent.

I always came away from the short, painful conversations acting like my inarticulate mumbling had not bothered me, but it had, every time. I did not know what else to do other than to keep trying. I had more determination than understanding about what I was seeking. I did not know how to fix my life; my imperfections seemed far too great. I finally convinced myself that maybe I had to become willing to engage in a better way of thinking, living, and behaving, so I could develop the desired skills needed to become a hearty, healthy, self-advocate.

I was finally able to speak with my mother respectfully by the late months of 1977. She in turn was grateful that I had found a way of living that I could build upon successfully, no matter what. She actually suggested I stay with whatever I had found that had helped me so much! This time, I understood her support; I had no animosity. That was one of the moments I'd wanted to live to experience; that's when I knew forgiveness was an equal opportunity, and I said, finally, "This is Good."

Chapter 15 - A Long Course in Miracles

First, a definition: *mir-a-cle* (mir'a-k'l), n. 1. A wonderful, inexplicable event; a wunderkind. 2. An event or effect in the physical world deviating from the known laws of nature.

I was exhausted from my many mental fights that no one could see or feel but me, but at last I felt a small degree of promise. It was so small I could have easily missed its magnetic power. I could have asked *who touched me* or what touched my sight, my mind, and my will, all at the same time. I knew, instinctively, that I had been altered by some supernatural power.

The morning of May 3, 1977, I awakened with a sense of energy that I had never felt before. This small but profound moment had begun the previous evening. In hindsight, this segment of the miracle started with being willing to not drink all day. At eight p.m. that night, I was introduced to a way of life that has worked for me for the past forty-one years. Once I recognized that my spiritual and natural tiredness was a sign of a deeper soul hunger, I began seeking for a cure like the devil was after me at full speed.

My previous attempts at finding a solution included sitting in one church pew after another, prescription and non-prescription medication, meditation, blaming, drinking, praying, crying, whining, psychics, therapists, counselors, relocations, psychological U-turns, lying to myself and you if you listened, and regurgitating bible verses galore. You name it, I'd tried as many old and new remedies as I could find or imagine. I was frightened and worn-out from my never-ending attempts to create a meaningful life. Between my boredom and my low energy existence, I didn't even have what it took to talk about my problem with anyone. Screaming for help was the only way I knew how to stand up to the seemingly unbeatable foe I carried within.

I am talking about the kind of exhaustion where you wake up every day without any pep and go to bed each night with the same dreary feeling. "When," I wondered daily, "did I get so doggone tired and bored?" I had not a clue. But at last I noticed my tedious tiredness was being removed one centimeter at a time. Finally, I understood: I had but one principal job in this life and that was (and still is) to take care of me and be available to support others whenever possible. For the first time in my thirty long years of living, I had set a goal. My goal was to erase my boredom and have a spirit lift, like a face lift. I wanted to acquire fundamental knowledge on releasing my heavy, pain-filled past, which I lugged around with me like a prized possession. I had to somehow shift into a more positive and desirable space, a space where I could focus on learning to live with light and love.

This new light way—at least new for me—was uncomfortable, and so unnerving. Changing my philosophy and acting upon the change at the same time took much practice. It's what most other people think of as a decent, typical way of living. I had to learn to think consciously and intentionally about how to live in the present, how to focus on experiencing each moment of change. I wanted to live a healthier life each day, rather than reliving the nightmare of my exhausted yesterdays.

For a long time, it was difficult to see or feel any signs of progress toward building a greater future for my children and myself. For many years, I'd asked myself "How can I break free of my tired, oppressed self? How can I move forward from agonizing over past experiences and conditions? I had serious doubts about whether there was any way to live in the present and stop living in the past!

Once I had set my goal, I became more aware of opportunities for growth. I would read or hear ideas that made sense that had never made sense before. At one point, someone suggested I come up with a code word to use whenever I reverted back to the past. I would say that word to myself as soon as I realized I was slipping back into old patterns of explaining. A little bit at a time, sometimes by the milliseconds, I would repeat my code word until my morbid focus on my past life and old ways of thinking finally disassociated with my new present. Verbally asking questions about my lack of energy was not enough to pry lose my stagnant past and cast it into the sea of "no more." I had once believed that approach could work. I now knew I had to work harder to achieve even single moments of present freedom. Now that I had so much less energy, I wondered how I would ever manage such a feat.

I understood my tomorrows would be healthier, happier, and more fulfilling as I learned more about thinking and acting independently of my past experiences. I needed to practice, to develop my self-actualization "muscles" until I was strong enough physically, mentally, and emotionally to work toward greater todays, to create glorious and more rewarding tomorrows. Happily, I did come up with a word – a two word phrase, to be more exact – which began to work instantly in my self-talk, to negate my past. I borrowed the two words from one of my heroes, Lisa Nichols, a renowned motivational speaker. The phrase was and still is: "Yes, Yes!"

I believe visiting one's unpleasant past from time to time can be instructive, but I began to see that constantly living in past unpleasantness simply created a life of unmitigated disaster. No one cares; everyone has a past they are bobbing and weaving, ducking and dodging, and avoiding. Today I am learning how to finally rest in the ongoing process of learning, and developing orderly, workable routines of healthy processes of living. For all that I have experienced, and all the physical and mental freedom I have finally achieved, I am grateful.

Thank you was the only prayer I could pray for a long time. When I was a small child, one of the many songs we used to sing was, "I Love the Lord, He Heard My Cry." Not a day has gone by without a *thank you,* uttered from my lips, or my mind, since my emotional deliverance was granted. The master of the universe heard my many cries of despair. My pain was so great in my early twenties that someone had suggested I read Psalm 116: 1-19. As I read it, I realized the Psalmist was giving instructions for me to follow. I read the chapter and studied each verse, and I finally found the key. I read it daily until I could digest the actions required to change my outlook on myself, my life, and my journey from past and present.

What were those instructions? First, know that God hears you and listens to you. Second, call upon God; tell him of your sorrows and troubles. Third, ask for help; plead for deliverance from your grief. Fourth, be grateful; show your gratitude in everything you do. And the rest: Spread your joy and happiness to others. Tell your story. Acknowledge the grace and glory of God when you tell your story. Help those who are suffering; let God work through you. Publicly vow to act as an agent of God, to help others, to make life better for those around you. Call upon God for the help you need, and then pay him back by gratefully helping those around you. Verse seventeen says, to "offer...the sacrifice...of thanksgiving." If that isn't a commandment to be grateful, I don't know what is.

Later, another person suggested studying the *Twelve Laws of the Universe* to help me find a balance with universal living and support while I was waiting for human help to show up. Studying the laws provided great insight. I first read through the laws themselves: The Law of Divine Oneness, The Law of Action, The Law of Correspondence, The Law of Cause and Effect, The Law of Compensation, The Law of Attraction, The Law of Perpetual Transmutation of Energy, The Law of Relativity, The Law of Polarity, The Law of Rhythm, and the Law of Gender. Some of the laws provided strength in knowledge; others provided practical daily understanding. Studying these laws seems to provide a sense of tremendous mental clarity and stability.

I have found that being still and being comfortable takes much practice and daily surrender. Developing better communication skills in order to recreate my story and express my forever loving gratitude will remain a work in progress. My fears still fight for their right to have a front row seat within my mind, but more and more often now, courage prevails. While my small steps still seem insignificant at times, faith and gratitude light my pathway today. Loving acts of kindness and selflessness have replaced my self-centeredness. Striving for change of character always reveals new challenges and new weaknesses, and sometimes shows unexplainable awkwardness when it comes to making independent choices for my good.

I constantly think about what I'm doing and remind myself that what is happening right now is real and the past is gone. I have noticed that as I gain new freedoms and make more positive changes in my life, my desire to develop deeper character-building skills increases, and my confusion and inner conflicts lessen. I can't say when I first felt the joys of being released from self-sabotaging behaviors and stresses, but I can say I feel that joy regularly now, and more predictably with each passing day.

Learning to release some of my fears has been noticeably rewarding. I am finally able to speak in public without emotional panic overwhelming me. As is true with public speaking and writing, I believe the ability to embrace emotional freedom requires its own kind of strength and produces its own kind of self-governing. As a matter of fact, through repetition and time, I've found a happier self and a higher level of contentment. Some may call this state "emotional maturity," or spiritual maturity.

Likewise, my newfound self-approval has taken precedence over the laughing-to-keep-from-crying façade I had employed in past years. My edgy, strained, fake laughter was arrested in the late sixties. Even then I knew enough to know fake was not me. But without a replacement for my fake, insincere behavior, I grew into an even more silent and ferocious self-critic. This feeling ate away at my soul. When I finally gained, in 1978, the ability to feel and hear authentic laughter from within for the first time I felt a great sense of hope; it literally shocked me. Little by little, my unnecessary burdens have been rolled away. Internally and externally, my many protective masks are no longer needed to guard me from thee.

Finally, I was able to focus on genuine restorative measures. When I once had only been able to prevent further damage, now I am able to work on finding solutions that allow me to live from the inside out. While I was learning new words, music, concepts, and coping skills, I also developed new behaviors that brought a comforting balm to my mind and my soul. Even my every-three-day physical appetite changed to wanting daily meals.

Creating my own happily-ever-after took more than patience and tender loving care; it took acceptance, and faith, and determination, until the change became a reality I could believe in. At long last, each moment in time, I simply learned to love ME. I learned to acknowledge my successes and look for ways to correct my failures. I now experience plenty of moments of what appears to be a genuine sense of self-worth in action. I know that failure – the act of making mistakes and learning from them – is the best teacher. Mistakes aren't reflections of worth; they are simply reflections of our efforts. If one makes mistakes it means one has made the attempt and identified a lesson to be corrected or accepted.

I can now look at my less-than-beautiful young growing up years of as my constant "school of hard knocks," as "my rocks in a weary land," as the old hymn goes. With a lot of missteps and giving up false perceptions along the way, I gradually learned new and effective life lessons and grew to appreciate the magnitude of what I had lived through and healed from.

These days, living in my new, healthy reality is a choice. My confidence now enfolds me like a chic silk dress. Finding a way to love myself has brought an empowering sense of accomplishment. I am so relieved and grateful to know that there was a way out of my emotional and physical dilemmas of living in ensnared chaos and – when I truly needed to find that path – it presented itself to me.

I continue to be an eager student in the classrooms of life. Most of my formal classes have focused on becoming a more loving human being. I've had to learn that change is not always easy and not always painless. Usually, it's neither of those things. Any rewards for changing, or for just tolerating the change process, go largely unnoticed by others. Supporting the healing journey, from being abused to making amends, from brokenness to being restored, and from battered to loveable, is a self-rewarding venture. It is simply a gift to self from a power greater than my own, to support those I am called to serve. I learned finally to just trust the many ongoing processes. My unloving roots have taught me to value loving methods of seeking and acquiring change. *Letting go* is one of those universal steps in the process of change.

My self-discipline skills are still a work in progress. Although I've learned to make sense of the life I was forced to lead as a child, I still have many days when I can make very little sense of what I endured growing up. Occasionally, though, I can totally understand the many struggles of my parents' lives and the challenges they faced in child rearing. Not making excuses, I reason that my parents were as ill-prepared for parenthood and adulthood as I was, possibly even more so. Many parenting programs, platforms, curriculum guides, and teaching tools have been designed to aid unprepared parents in their struggle with healthy family assistance, even birth control methods. Some of those aids were not available in those early days of my life or my parents' lives, just as new support systems are continuingly being developed as I write today.

I now realize that with steady determination I can make my life one of success, financial and otherwise. Renewing my outlook each day makes life more orderly, both for me and for those I am endeavoring to serve. A part of my personal vision was to continue to gain a greater sense of self-worth and natural peace, to expand my self-awareness, and to have an exuberant sense of exhilaration. All of these things have happened and more. I have even learned to hug!

I've learned that good nutrition, proper rest, and healthy connection with others are all essential to a continuum of professional and personal growth. As an adult, being aware of what is in front of me and knowing I have the strength to obtain it, keeps me from obsessively looking over my shoulder at my past failures. The awareness of a new and different way of breathing, examining, and stretching encourages me to stumble forward no matter what.

What I now know for sure is this: genuine lasting change requires a plan of action and deep conviction. Finally understanding the need for self-leadership skills has allowed me to go through new learning processes without unnecessary dithering. I have also come to know that complete understanding is not always necessary in order to make healthy decisions. Change for me sometimes is akin to blind but persistent stumbling through financial, emotional, and spiritual challenges using makeshift processes, lesson plans, and methods towards greater self-control and peace.

I had become comfortable with the talk of going somewhere, but it was often just talk. I learned that talk is not just cheap, it is actually free. It doesn't mean a thing unless you back it up with determination and action. Genuine change requires action, action, and more action.

For so long, I let my many fears tell me what to think, how to behave and misbehave, what to do, where to go, what to feel, when to go, what mask to wear on each trip, and how often to change masks. I was apparently more gifted at unwittingly minimizing acts of faith, and – again, unwittingly – maximizing fear-based notions.

In the beginning, changing, shifting, from old negative behaviors to energizing healthy behaviors was very difficult. I found it tough to love either myself or anyone else. I long believed it was because I had never been loved, but that turned out to be not quite the whole truth. In the initial stages of learning to shift, it was easier for me to find fault or discredit any progress made than it was to consistently practice new behaviors or work at changing my mindset. Maintaining even the smallest increments of new, healthy routine practices was irritating and frustrating. Embracing new behaviors was challenging without a coach, or a mentor. I would have truly benefitted from a life support group. Creating new pathways of thinking and living felt strange and intolerable. The transition of learning new and unfamiliar steps, stages, and processes to overcome my past habits felt awkward and made me reluctant to practice. I was afraid of failure. I felt conspicuous and incompetent when I was learning new behaviors. Once I gained even a glimmer of true self-love and its many languages and behaviors, all the old excuses lost their power against the force of being more loving and practicing the new and better ways of functioning. When love is served, it is service at its finest.

As I write, I still must work to limit my all-too-readily-available inclination to whine and complain, and I know despite my best efforts it manages to slip in sometimes. Nevertheless, learning from the heavy crosses and crowns of thorns that defined my earlier life has proven rewarding at last. I learned to get involved with recreating my life's story; that is my responsibility.

Rewriting my story to see its beauty and benefits has been phenomenal and paramount. My parents were a part of the second great migration from 1940 to 1970; they were not alone in their desperation to find better ways to survive. Neither of my parents had more than a third-grade education; moving from the farm to the city may have posed even more difficult challenges for them. I can still remember my mother raising chickens in the city. It was an economic necessity for her, something I could see and understand even then. I've learned first-hand the price to be paid for raising one's family without having the rudiments of dignity, self-love, and integrity already instilled within to draw upon during demanding times.

I can see now what I could not see then: I started rewriting my own story, one tiny step at a time, almost unconsciously. My need to survive and thrive outweighed my need to remain anxiously but comfortably miserable. I took my first step toward switching life paths in 1971 when I began to have a yearning to further my academic education. Without knowing what I was doing, I subconsciously fell into a pattern of being employed as long as I could tolerate the discomfort of being employed, and then, once I was unemployed again, I would create a remedy for the discomfort by signing up for a class at the local college. The cycle of being employed and unemployed sporadically for short spells was taking its toll on me. Enrolling in a business course of some sort was something I could manage to do, to finish successfully. Although I could not see far enough down the road to predict the ultimate outcome, it seemed like a worthwhile pattern, and over the long term, it worked. These courses generally were six months in duration – not too long for me to be able to stick with them to the finish, even though my depression and frustrations seemed permanently and forever present. As I attended one class after another this process made my inability to remain employed more tolerable. No matter what job I had, I seemed to lack the ability to stay on the job and felt compelled to quit again and again. My protective instincts urged me to take classes and do whatever else I could do to make my life livable, even with my disadvantage of having so many missing basic skills.

I could not see it happening when I started, but after a few years of taking classes I was able to earn my GED certificate in 1974. Although I knew in my mind that this was a great achievement, it still brought with it more disappointment than a feeling of accomplishment. In my heart, it seemed like I was still just making up for lost time and not gaining any momentum to keep moving forward. I was frustrated: I wanted to leap over the barriers and catapult forward to the point where I felt I should be. I didn't know it then, but now I know why it took me so long: I wasn't ready. One of the biggest lessons I had to learn through all of this was *patience*. Growth generally comes in steps, not in great leaps.

In moments of creativity, self-leadership must remain the driving force, rather than the paralyzing fear. If faced with equally appealing (or even equally unappealing) options, sometimes there is no clear answer. Choose one: if it works out, great; if not, find another. Overcoming decision-making impairments was one of my biggest hurdles.

I continued to work as long as I could and attended courses to develop more academic, social, and emotional skills. In 1976, as a metro driver in Texas, I was still searching for a window of opportunity, but it eluded me yet again. I was still not ready. I still had demons to vanquish. When those demons threatened to get the better of me, I resigned eight months later and returned to Kansas City, Missouri in March 1977.

I found employment briefly when I arrived back in KC, then got thirsty again, and found drinking more appealing than accountability and commitment. My intention was to drink and work, to drink and live, to drink, and be happy, but it never quite worked out that way. As a matter of fact, it was the total opposite: drink and be miserable, drink and be unmotivated (spiritually dead), drink and embrace self-pity, drink and be without the will to want to be employed, drink and be sadder, drink some more. It seemed that I just wanted to drink and drink and drink some more. This was how it worked out. At last, on that miraculous night, I saw my reality with drinking. I lost that job as easily as I had found it. I began to reflect again on my unquenchable thirst for alcohol. In May 1977, my obsessive thirst for alcohol was at last quenched. My need to drink was arrested. Finally, I learned the true meaning of steps, stages, and processes. I needed to eliminate the obvious stumbling blocks and turn my stumbling blocks into stepping stones if I wanted to improve my life. With tears in my eyes, I said goodbye to an illusionary way of life that offered no comfort and no healthy rewards.

For many years, I had walked on and off one job after another as if I did not know any better. My emotional make-up would not allow me to tarry too long at any one position. Once my desire for drinking was removed in 1977, I held my next job for eighteen solid months. That victory was one of my first modern-day miracles. In 1979, I resigned from that miracle job, cautiously, for a greater opportunity with the Division of Family Services. I remained there for the next six years. That was another victory on my modern-day miracles list. I had finally learned how to find salvation in the basic rudiments of employment.

In 1985, I resigned from DFS and relocated to the State of Washington, where I enrolled in a six-month computer class. After completing the class, I became employed with the University of Washington in 1986. Twelve years later, in 1998, while still working at UW, I took on an additional full-time position with the Walmart Company. I also enrolled in school at Evergreen State College at the end of that year, in December 1998. I earned my Bachelor of Arts degree in 2003, while working both jobs full time. I remained at UW until 2008 and stayed with Walmart until 2009. As I continued to look at my personal growth accomplishments, there was still so much knowledge, and so many skills, tools, and abilities yet missing. I was still bothered by too many ineffective, nonproductive thoughts and actions. I was still letting negative behavioral patterns lead me instead of practicing behaviors that would allow me to be led by positive, regenerative thinking more than by potentially destructive actions.

One of my many desires was to learn to improve my writing skills. I transferred to a job with a company that allowed me the luxury to hand write a daily report for the next five to eight years. I took on another part-time job and remained in both positions for eight years. I was amazed by how wanting a comma behind my name held me in school for six amazing years, how powerful that desire was in keeping me on task! I promised myself if I ever wrote a book, I wanted a comma behind my last name. What an awesome manifestation: the power of a tiny comma. Wow! *Release Me*, by Leona P. Jackson, B.A.

In the end I found true passion. I've also learned that a love that comes from within is not easily compromised. Once, not long ago, my useless energy would not allow me to withstand the bitter stings of disharmony; now my courage allows me the energy of harmony to shift my mindset with understanding and enthusiasm. Some may call it a sense of feeling whole or making the most of the Law of Vibration.

I now find surprising rewards of gratitude when I am able to effectively handle or resolve difficult situations to the satisfaction of all involved. This is a new skill – one I never had when I was younger – and I am so grateful to be able to help myself and others in this way.

I do this by a combination of drawing on the cosmos to maintain higher frequencies mixed with the Law of Rhythm or any of the other eleven laws that makes sense. I never dreamed growth opportunities would present themselves so readily. I never dreamed of being grateful for growth opportunities at all, but I have learned that having an attitude of thankfulness often strengthens my inner team. I am no longer skeptical of this mystical source, for it has performed a great change within me. I am no longer waiting for others or for a Greater Power to do for me what I can do for myself. I am amazed by the awesome feeling that sometimes success comes from just choosing to let go.

This does not mean I have found a handbook on how to let go of things I can't change. What it does mean is now I know I have the power to choose, and that knowledge is a priceless gift. I have learned that once I become *willing* to let go, the useless fighting stops and letting go becomes a feeling of desire. Being willing to let go is probably ninety-nine percent of the battle. I have learned how to let go of ineffective behaviors and attitudes. The unhealthy me I once knew finally became so uncomfortable that I had to find a better way. Letting go of old ideas became the better way for me.

I finally comprehended the steps I needed to take to take charge and change my life. I am still mastering those steps, treasuring each stage as a precious moment in my life. I'm gauging my progress not against who I thought other people expected me to be, or who I used to think I was supposed to be, but against who I used to be, how far I've come, and who I desire to be. My goal, and my desire, is to be nothing short of an evolving person. I have come far enough now that I can – at last – envision individual elements of self-empowerment.

Changing the things that need to be changed, and that I *can* change, is now the dominating mandate in my life. To facilitate this obligation, exercising self-discipline has made its way onto my daily agenda. Today I know the power of prioritizing, prayer, manifesting, meditation, goal setting, and being honest with myself. Where I only originally desired to have a sense of ease and comfort, to gain confidence and to be bodacious, today I am more than I set out to be oh-so-many-years ago.

Along the way, I had to educate myself about mental health, learning styles, nutrition, fitness, personal and business communications, time and money management, and a dozen other topics that can impact my daily existence. The topic of mental illness now has a protected, reserved, and valued place at the table for insight, dialogue, and discussion, along with wellness practices, professional pursuits, personal care, and spirituality

Once I had gained a vocabulary sufficient to allow me to participate in the language of discourse in a few given fields, I also found the willingness and the ability to dump my long-running fallback excuse, "It wasn't my fault." I was able to rearrange my thinking to a much more productive default statement, "It is my responsibility to live a noteworthy life. No one else can do that for me!" But first I had to find my own authentic value. I could not do this alone, and I did not always know where to look for help, but invariably, whenever I truly needed it and to my utter amazement, help came, time and time again, mostly from strangers.

My life now feels validated with purpose, healthy relationships, and a commitment to ongoing personal development. My priorities are healthy as far as family ties go. Finally having adequate emotional and spiritual development is another modern day miracle for me.

I continue to work at increasing better skills relating to financial control and economic freedom. Becoming more aware of the lessons I have learned helps me to exercise wisdom when it comes to staying focused on my priorities. I still continually pursue educational opportunities; I can never learn too much. My desire to keep learning defines my boundaries: now that I am finally in the business of restructuring and creating my life with intent and as growth circumstances present themselves, rather than waiting for life to happen to me, I am not about to stop!

My relentless search for answers and my efforts of trying to redirect my inner compass finally took hold and helped me to see how I could mold my previously painful, stressful, and unsatisfactory life into a life worth living. What was once deep self-loathing and self-deception has developed into an equally deep self-respect and a clear conscience. My concerted effort to shift from living a life of consumption and chaos to living a life of service to others brings me great joy.

I am still amazed at the difference it can make to just decide to have a *can change* attitude. To finally be *enough* now seems normal. For the joyous life I live today, the words I've written, the mental and physical freedom I've finally achieved, I am grateful! I hope to spend the rest of my life giving back what has been so freely and generously given to me. I meditate upon these words, "Pass It On!"

The biggest lesson of all, the key takeaway, is that I am a reaction to what I am connected to. If I am plugged in to hate, or anger, or fear, that's what I act or react with. On the other hand, if I am connected to the energy giver, I operate with and through my divine purpose. Learning this single, key principle finally allowed me to understand what my primary mistake had been for so long.

My primary mistake was this: I believed, subconsciously, that if I did not understand the natural and spiritual laws, then I was exempt from learning or practicing new and different, productive behaviors. It's amazing what we sometimes rationalize, just to avoid the responsibility of clear, valid, thinking and doing.

Somewhere along my journey, I ran into the idea that challenging the status-quo and problem solving, and producing results are common leadership expectations, but the highest calling of leadership is to unlock potential in others." I don't know the source for the idea, so I can't cite it here, but the idea of helping others to unlock their potential resonates loudly with me.

As I read and re-read this quote earlier in my life, I often wondered who would help me and when would that unknown person unlock the potential in me? Was I not someone worthy of receiving help from others? As I became more observant, I found that many people lack the confidence to share any real substantial support or assistance, and the ones who were officially qualified to do so were often too busy. I also realized that more help may have been available to me than I knew, and that I had to be ready to learn, and ready to accept help, before having it available would be useful to me.

Finally, after waiting by the pool of "Will Somebody Please Help Me" for thirty long years, I understood that I had but one principal job in this life: it was my job to take care of me and to be available to support others when possible. Just like every other person on this planet, I get an awesome opportunity to enlarge my natural and spiritual condition, not just on any one day but every single day. I get to celebrate my progress on a different level, thanks to the many excellent opportunities that have come my way. Every time I receive evidence that all is well with my soul; I have a little spiritual celebration.

I have found it helpful to adopt a motto for my life as I go along. That motto changes periodically as I grow and my priorities shift. Today my motto is: *More Divine and Less Whine.*

As I meditate on it and incorporate the idea of "less whining" into my life, I find I see things differently, and seeing any issue from a different perspective can change how I respond to it. For a very long time, I believed that if I was afraid of something that I should avoid it. Fear stopped me at almost every turn. Then I came across this idea, from Eleanor Roosevelt: "Believe in yourself. You gain strength, courage, and confidence by every experience in which you stop to look fear in the face. ...You must do that which you think you cannot do."

This was a belief-shattering idea to me, but it allowed me to take a closer and different look at how I was living. I suddenly became aware of how much one's perspective can affect what one sees and understands.

One incident in particular from my own life had a powerful impact on my thinking: My son and daughter and I took an Amtrak to Kansas City, Missouri from Albuquerque, New Mexico. I was going to leave the children with family in Missouri while I returned to New Mexico to finish my data entry class. I had a week or so to go before the class ended but I became overly anxious to leave. It bothered me that I started projects and didn't complete them for no other reason than my own restlessness. I made sure my children were safe, and then I flew back to New Mexico to finish my class. It seemed so important to me, at the time, to finish what I had started.

After I completed the class and received my certificate, I returned to Kansas City. My life was so hectic and chaotic, going here and there, running from one thing and place to the next. As the plane made its approach to Kansas City, I looked out the window and was amazed by how neat and organized everything on the ground appeared to be. From that overhead distance, everything appeared to be in orderly sections, tidy, serene. I had never viewed anything that gave me such a dramatic alternative perspective on living my life.

As I gazed down at the city, as I studied the organized view from above, my mind opened just a little bit, and my heart opened just a little bit, and I thought maybe, just maybe, I could get my life together. Maybe, just maybe, I could find a way to eliminate the chaos. It was a true moment of disorder shifting into orderly precision. That moment led to many more moments like it, and ultimately to my ability to intentionally make choices and decisions based on my own confidence and belief in myself and my divine capabilities. The most profound of all those decisions was the one that led me, more than forty years later, to write this book, and to share these lessons with you.

Psalms, Chapter 116

1 I love the LORD, because he hath heard my voice *and* my supplications.

2 Because he hath inclined his ear unto me, therefore will I call upon *him* as long as I live.

3 The sorrows of death compassed me, and the pains of hell gat hold upon me: I found trouble and sorrow.

4 Then called I upon the name of the LORD; O LORD, I beseech thee, deliver my soul.

5 Gracious *is* the LORD, and righteous; yea, our God *is* merciful.

6 The LORD preserveth the simple: I was brought low, and he helped me.

7 Return unto thy rest, O my soul; for the LORD hath dealt bountifully with thee.

8 For thou hast delivered my soul from death, mine eyes from tears, *and* my feet from falling.

9 I will walk before the LORD in the land of the living.

10 I believed, therefore have I spoken: I was greatly afflicted:

11 I said in my haste, all men *are* liars.

12 What shall I render unto the LORD *for* all his benefits toward me?

13 I will take the cup of salvation, and call upon the name of the LORD.

14 I will pay my vows unto the LORD now in the presence of all his people.

15 Precious in the sight of the LORD *is* the death of his saints.

16 O LORD, truly I *am* thy servant; I *am* thy servant, *and* the son of thine handmaid: thou hast loosed my bonds.

17 I will offer to thee the sacrifice of thanksgiving, and will call upon the name of the LORD.

18 I will pay my vows unto the LORD now in the presence of all his people,

19 In the courts of the LORD'S house, in the midst of thee, O Jerusalem. Praise ye the LORD.

The Power of Attitude

"Our lives are not determined by what happens to us, but how we react to what happens. Not by what life brings to us, but by the attitude we bring to life.
A positive attitude causes a chain reaction of positive thoughts, events, and outcomes. It is a catalyst . . . a spark that creates extraordinary results."

~Mac Anderson

Afterword

During my spinning top years, I'd watched this energetic person, my mother, always on the go and in a hurry going somewhere, always doing something different and facing challenges galore. I wondered if she would ever slow down and take it easy. I wondered if I would survive being in this endless super hectic environment. I wondered how I would fit in as I sat pushing my spinning top trying to see just how fast it would go. My mother reminded me of my spinning top, spinning at max speed out of control and yet spinning from pumped up energy, in control. Up until the time I left home, I do not remember my mother ever sitting still. She was forever going, coming, and changing her mind in mid-stream, like her mental signals were continually switching between stop and go. I was more of a relaxed person myself; I could not see for the life of me what all of the hurrying was all about. She would do her chores around the house while listening to Eddie Kendricks singing *Shoeshine Boy* and *Keep on Trucking*.

Later on, she reminded me more of a drill sergeant. While she was changing plans, she screamed a lot with each command. "Put this on," "hurry up," "brush your hair," "go there," and "come-hither" all day long. *I calmly informed her one day that I could not do all of that nonstop.* Between her many jobs and our new addresses, it was mass confusion going around in circles. While she was changing jobs, I was changing schools. I had always believed we were taking mini vacations like everyone else, only we took many more of them. I was small; I loved it. We would move to another address in or out of town. I was an introvert and the frequent moves meant I didn't know anyone nearby, so I didn't need to worry about conversing with the many new faces who came in and out of my life.

After I graduated from high school, I joined the Army Reserve. In her too busy schedule with my sister and me, and her always having two or three jobs to keep up with, she still always found time to write letters. She sometimes wrote daily, sometimes weekly, or she even made phone calls while I was away. This was my first time away from home; it should have been a wonderful adventure, but it wasn't. As I faced a real drill sergeant for the first time, I realized I was not up for the challenge. Somehow, I survived. Her letters to me during this time also meant I was reading her writing for the first time. Those letters were a comfort to me.

In the end, this complex, constantly-in-motion woman learned to function with remarkable order and efficiency. I am not surprised that she has written her first book. I am, however, surprised that she could sit still long enough to write words of peace and understanding. Another miracle!

Her unscripted thoughts, as well as our vast experiences as a family, have served us well. My mother is a thinker of many thoughts; I could understand that by simple observation. I believe her writing this book is one of her utmost rewarding endeavors thus far; I hope she will bless us with another book very soon.

Right on, LPJ!
Richard B. Charles

A NOTE FROM THE AUTHOR

Thank you for taking the time to read *RELEASE ME!* If you love what you've read, please leave a brief review on your favorite online reader review site.

To find out about my upcoming projects, be sure to subscribe to my newsletter by sending a message with "sign me up!" in the subject line to:

Leonasbooks@gmail.com

Visit my Facebook page: http://facebook.com/LeonaPJackson

SNEAK PREVIEW

Leona's next project is well under way. Turn the page for a sneak preview!

Coming soon!

Financial Fitness: Becoming un-messy with Money, by Leona P. Jackson, BA

Are you messy with money? For many years, I was, too.

Introduction

After working so desperately in my family's business for eleven years, I was – among other insufficiencies – financially starved by not receiving any pay whatsoever. I have spent the better part of my adult life trying to understand and satisfy that resentment of not being good enough to be paid for my work. Because it was my own parents who had so little respect for me, my negative feelings about money were compounded and commingled with my feelings about family, love, and relationships; that's a very complicated way to relate to your resources!

For many years, I craved having money to spend, much the same way one might crave chocolate, or alcohol, or cigarettes. That craving for spending far outweighed the craving or need for sound financial planning or developing healthy saving or budgeting habits. As I conquered my other demons, one at a time, I slowly became aware of how tangled up my thinking about money had become, and how complicated it was going to be to get untangled.

I realized I needed to know more about how money and finances and physical and emotional reality worked and didn't work together before I could begin to build a functional financial life for myself. As I studied, I discovered that I needed to be aware of numerous factors that can impact our individual approach to money:

1. The Fact of Financial Life Cycles
2. The Influence of Financial Beliefs
3. The Power of Financial Attitude

4. The Importance of Understanding and Following Financial Steps

4. The Importance of Understanding and Following Financial Steps
5. The Benefit of Financial Fluency
6. The Need for Financial Intuition
7. The Practicality of Financial Strength
8. The Force of Financial Faith
9. The Reality of Abundance
10. The Sensibility of Manifestation
11. The Potency of Financial Forgiveness
12. The Necessity of Saving
13. The Blessing of Budgeting
14. The Productivity of Planning
15. The Usefulness of Financial Analysis
16. The Skill of Strategic Thinking

In *Financial Fitness*, each of the above factors gets its own chapter discussion of its role in our financial universe and how the presence or absence of that factor can lead to success or failure in money-related matters.

I invite you to follow along as I detail my own financial education and growth, and explain how to work through the process yourself to nurture your own economic well-being.

Made in the USA
Columbia, SC
16 June 2019